Contents

Understanding Affirmative Action

Understanding Affirmative Action

Politics, Discrimination, and the Search for Justice

J. Edward Kellough

Washington, D.C.
Georgetown University Press

As of January 1, 2007, 13-digit ISBN numbers will replace the current 10-digit system.
Paperback: 978-1-58901-089-5

Georgetown University Press, Washington, D.C.

This book is printed on acid-free paper meeting the requirements of the American National Standard for Permanence in Paper for Printed Library Materials.

Library of Congress Cataloging-in-Publication Data

Kellough, J. Edward
   Understanding affirmative action : politics, discrimination, and the search for justice /
J. Edward Kellough.
      p. cm.
   Includes bibliographical references and index.
   ISBN-13: 978-1-58901-089-5 (pbk. : alk. paper)
   ISBN-10: 1-58901-089-2 (pbk. : alk. paper)
1. Affirmative action programs—Law and legislation—United States.
2. Affirmative action programs in education—Law and legislation—United States.
3. Affirmative action programs—United States. I. Title.
   KF4755.5.K45 2006
   342.7308'7—dc22   2005027243

13 12 11 10 09 08 07 06   9 8 7 6 5 4 3 2
First printing

Printed in the United States of America

Acknowledgments

This work has been informed by the scholarship of numerous individuals whose research is cited here. I am deeply grateful to those scholars for their contributions to our knowledge of affirmative action and its history. I am also grateful to the many students and colleagues whose discussions with me on the topics covered in this book have been extremely valuable. The manuscript was improved as a result of those conversations. I want to thank also the colleagues who read all or part of the manuscript while it was in preparation and offered suggestions for its improvement. They gave generously of their time and are much appreciated. Of course, all errors of fact or judgment that remain are entirely my own. Finally, I want to thank my wife, Vicki, and my sons, John and Eric, for their patience and encouragement as I finished this project. Their love and support have enriched my life beyond words. This book is dedicated to them.

Understanding Affirmative Action

one

Affirmative Action
The Concept and the Controversy

"Affirmative action" is a term familiar to most Americans but one not always well understood. Over time, it has signified a variety of strategies designed to enhance employment, educational, or business opportunities for groups, such as racial or ethnic minorities and women, who have suffered discrimination. However, the manner in which these efforts are implemented, the types of action they require, and the broader implications they carry for our society may vary from one specific program to another. The purpose of this book is to examine the concept of affirmative action, to review its history, to consider the different approaches undertaken, and to evaluate arguments offered by proponents and opponents. As is widely known, affirmative action has been one of the most controversial and divisive issues ever placed on the national agenda in the United States. People disagree on whether affirmative action should be permitted or, if it is judged to be necessary, on the specific types of efforts that should be included. The argument has continued in one form or another since the policy began over four decades ago.[1]

The persistent nature of the debate over affirmative action is indicative of the policy's significant implications. Alternative interpretations of such fundamental values as justice and equality lie at the heart of the dispute. Employment, educational, and business prospects are at stake, not only for groups targeted to benefit from the policy, but also for others who wish to compete for a share of those opportunities. The importance of the issues raised by affirmative action requires us to examine the policy with care. To understand it, readers must know how the policy originated and evolved, must recognize what affirmative action requires in various instances and what it does not require, must strive to understand arguments on both sides of the debate, and must be alert to separate fact from fiction.

As will be discussed in more detail in chapter 3 of this book, the middle and later years of the 1990s proved to be a particularly difficult time for those who supported affirmative action. Forces arrayed in opposition pressed their concerns with increasing vigor and success.[2] In November 1996, for example, voters in California approved Proposition 209, the widely known state constitutional amendment banning affirmative action policies that involved preferences for minorities and women in state employment, contracting, and university admissions. Two years later, in November 1998, a similar measure (I-200) was passed in the state of Washington, and additional ballot initiatives were planned in other states.[3] In 1999, Governor Jeb Bush of Florida issued an executive order eliminating affirmative action preferences in state contracts and employment and requesting the Board of Regents of the State University System to implement a similar policy regarding admissions to state institutions of higher education.[4]

As the 1990s came to a close, some observers concluded that affirmative action had run its course and that it would not survive long into the new century. Support for affirmative action had certainly eroded. A growing number of economically and socially conservative leaders in public office had voiced their opposition to the policy, and proposals to limit the use of affirmative action were raised in Congress and in numerous state legislative assemblies.[5] Politically motivated law firms also emerged to attack affirmative action in the courts, where their arguments often were well received.[6]

The federal judiciary, shaped to a considerable extent by appointments made by the Reagan and Bush administrations in the 1980s and early 1990s, ruled against affirmative action in a number of important cases. In 1995, for example, the U.S. Supreme Court, in *Adarand Constructors v. Pena*, significantly tightened constraints on the federal government's affirmative action policies by requiring they be subjected to strict judicial scrutiny.[7] In 1996, the U.S. Court of Appeals for the Fifth Circuit, in *Hopwood v. State of Texas*, ruled that the circumstances that would permit preferential forms of affirmative action by a state university were exceedingly narrow.[8] The circuit court struck down an affirmative action program that gave a limited preference to minority applicants at the University of Texas School of Law. Later, the U.S. Supreme Court refused to take the case under review, thus allowing the circuit court decision to stand without officially endorsing the ruling.[9]

Efforts by courts to tighten legal restrictions, and other steps taken to oppose affirmative action in the 1990s and thereafter, were consistent with the view that because progress by racial and ethnic minorities and women was made in previous decades, affirmative action was no longer necessary.[10] Nevertheless, others argued that discrimination and its effects had not been eradicated; that women and minorities were still underrepresented in higher-level positions in most organizations; and that affirmative action programs designed to assist these groups were, and are, still needed.[11]

It is impossible to know with certainty what the future will hold for affirmative action. To develop a better understanding of the policy and the dispute associated with it, however, three basic, but often neglected, facts should be considered.

1. A variety of policy options are in place that legitimately bear the label "affirmative action." Care should be taken to recognize such variation in discussions of the policy. As will be seen, different approaches to affirmative action have vastly different implications for concepts such as non-discrimination and equal opportunity.

2. Affirmative action, regardless of its specific form, is primarily a policy intended to promote the redistribution of opportunity. Some people benefit directly, while others may not be as well off as they would have otherwise been. Many arguments are offered on each side in the affirmative action debate, but readers should remember that the policy is essentially about who wins and who loses in the distribution of valued resources, and that reality is frequently what motivates those who press the debate most vociferously. The struggle over affirmative action is truly a political contest consistent with Harold D. Lasswell's classic definition of politics as "who gets what, when, and how."[12]

3. The legal foundation for affirmative action, as it has been articulated by the courts, cannot be understood unless it is reviewed systematically

and pains are taken to distinguish cases on the basis of the different settings in which affirmative action occurs, as well as the precise nature of the underlying legal challenges. For example, arguments made to defend affirmative action in employment and higher education contexts are different in important ways. In employment settings, arguments often focus on the need for an equitable distribution of opportunities. In educational admissions programs, those arguments are present, but the focus is also on the educational value of having a diverse student body. In addition, challenges to affirmative action can be made on the basis of statutory law or, if a public authority is involved, on the basis of the U.S. Constitution. A failure to distinguish between the specific forms of the policy, and the legal bases for challenges to it, makes the process of trying to clearly define the boundaries of legally permissible affirmative action nearly impossible.

The Variety of Approaches to Affirmative Action

Confusion over the desirability and legality of affirmative action programs often stems from the fact that the policy can take a number of forms. For example, affirmative action may consist of efforts that emphasize recruitment and outreach activities designed to increase the diversity of applicant pools. In the area of employment, career development or upward mobility programs may be intended to provide opportunities to lower-level workers, a disproportionate number of whom are members of minority groups or women. Even efforts to keep track of the numbers of minorities or women within an organization may be considered a preliminary form of affirmative action. Other approaches involve the establishment of numerical goals and timetables for the representation of women and minorities and call for the consideration of factors such as sex and race in actual selection decisions.

Minority recruitment and outreach characterized as affirmative action was first pursued in a significant manner in the context of equal employment opportunity in the 1960s. Executive Order 10925, issued by President John F. Kennedy in 1961, required federal government contractors to "take affirmative action to ensure that applicants are employed and that employees are treated during employment without regard to their race, creed, color, or national origin."[13] In practice, this language meant that businesses with federal contracts were not expected to simply avoid discrimination against minority applicants or employees, but were directed to actively encourage their employment. Kennedy's order also required federal departments and agencies to take similar "affirmative steps" to realize the national policy of nondiscrimination in the civil service. President Lyndon B. Johnson's Executive Order 11246, issued in 1965, reasserted the affirmative action requirements of the Kennedy order.[14]

In contrast to these general outreach efforts, numerical goals and timetables for minority employment began to appear in affirmative action plans in the late 1960s and early in the 1970s. Later, they also were developed to assist women. Numerical goals are targets for the representation of minorities and women in an organization. Timetables set dates or timeframes within which goals are scheduled to be accomplished. Although goals and timetables do not require an organization to select individuals who fail to possess requisite qualifications, they do imply that, other things being equal, minority group members or women will be preferred.

The impetus for development of affirmative action goals and timetables was the excruciatingly slow rate of progress made by minorities and women under earlier approaches and the perception by many observers that the problem was grave enough that an alternative strategy was necessary.[15] Indeed, the use of goals and timetables represented a significant policy change from earlier strategies precisely because they are formulated on the basis of race, ethnicity, and sex, and efforts to achieve them may include the extension of preferences to qualified minorities or women. As a result, selection policies designed to achieve specified goals are not strictly neutral. As might be expected, this "nonneutral" approach is the form of affirmative action that has spawned the most substantial controversy and judicial activity. In fact, the controversy over numerical goals and timetables has been so widely expressed that preferences directed toward groups such as minorities and women have become synonymous with the concept of affirmative action in the minds of most people. Nathan Glazer, a forceful critic of preferential affirmative action in the late 1980s observed that "there is no point arguing with what the meaning of the words has become: whatever the term meant in the 1960s, since the 1970s affirmative action means quotas and goals and timetables."[16]

Recruitment and outreach programs have, nevertheless, remained vital components of affirmative action policy over the years. Glazer, however, equated affirmative action exclusively with goals and timetables, and by using the term "quotas," he implied that when affirmative action is pursued, employment or other opportunities are restricted to groups such as minorities or women, or that a specific number or percentage of minority group members or women will be brought into an organization, regardless of merit. Glazer's comments highlight arguments widely shared and often adopted by those opposed to the policy.

Supporters of affirmative action reject Glazer's view. From their perspective, minority or female employment goals are objectives that an organization endeavors to achieve alongside many other aspirations. Affirmative action goals should in no way be associated with lowering basic qualifications standards. For example, an organization may plan to hire an identified number of minority applicants provided that sufficiently qualified individuals can be found, and to achieve that goal, it may engage in targeted outreach to ensure that enough qualified minorities apply; standards that allow or condone the selection of unqualified individuals are never contemplated. Numerical targets such as this have been included in affirmative action programs of various organizations for years. No statute, regulation, or court requires employers to hire or promote unqualified people. Indeed, the burden on employers or other organizations to meet specified goals has always been limited legally by the availability of qualified applicants.[17] In this sense, quotas to favor the unqualified have never been sanctioned.

Opponents of affirmative action goals and preferences are likely to respond that if such devices do not favor selection of the unqualified, they may nevertheless lead to the appointment of individuals who are *less* qualified. This can be a valid criticism. However, this argument assumes that measures of qualifications will be accurate enough to permit a precise assessment of varying degrees of ability. Sometimes that type of assessment may be possible, but more often knowing with certainty the exact level of qualifications held by individuals who have all been judged to meet acceptable standards is difficult. It is possible, nevertheless, that preferential affirmative action may produce outcomes in which talented and able persons who are not the most highly qualified are selected.

No end to this debate is likely. Opponents of preferential affirmative action often choose the term "quotas" to describe numerical strategies for the selection of women and minorities. One might recall, for example, George H. W. Bush (U.S. president from 1989 to 1993) originally referred to legislation that ultimately culminated in the Civil Rights Act of 1991 as a "quota bill."[18] The President vetoed an early version of that legislation in 1990.[19] The argument made by those with this point of view is that while affirmative action may not *require* an erosion of qualification standards, an erosion of standards is what often happens in practice when jobs or other valued positions are distributed, at least in part, on the basis of race, ethnicity, or sex. Proponents of affirmative action point out, however, that numerical targets for the selection of minorities or women should be set only after an organization develops a projection of the number of vacancies or other opportunities expected to be available and estimates the number of legitimately qualified minorities or women in potential applicant pools. This approach to affirmative action is nothing more, they argue, than an adaptation of the common management practice of responding to a problem by setting an objective and planning for its accomplishment.[20] Such policies often are intended to serve the remedial purpose of correcting the effects of past or current patterns of discrimination against minorities and women, but they can also operate to promote other advantages that may be associated with greater racial, ethnic, or gender diversity within an organization.

Given the continuing dispute over affirmative action policies involving goals and preferences, the relationship between such policies and efforts to promote equality of opportunity begs clarification. Affirmative action, including those programs with established goals and timetables, is conceived as part of larger attempts to promote equality of opportunity. Equal opportunity programs generally rest on a foundation of policy statements prohibiting discrimination. However, a policy prohibiting discrimination alone may be little more than an expression of sentiment. Additional procedures may be needed to effectively combat discriminatory practices directed toward minorities and women. One such procedure calls for the investigation of complaints of discrimination. Under a complaint processing system, organizational officials respond to allegations of discrimination brought to their attention by those who believe they have been denied equality of opportunity. The underlying concept is that opportunity should not be withheld because of characteristics such as race, ethnicity, sex, and religion. Efforts to ensure equality of opportunity are designed to prevent and overcome intentional and nonintentional discrimination against minorities, women, and other groups that have been victimized historically.

The burden for initiating a complaint, however, rests on the individual or individuals who have been subjected to discrimination. Because many such individuals are hesitant to register complaints, especially when confronted with discriminatory environments and the possibility of retaliation, policies based on complaint processing have often proved to be of limited utility. This was especially the case when this approach was first developed in the 1940s and 1950s, but it may continue even today. Indeed, the relatively slow pace of change that was produced when antidiscrimination policy rested primarily on complaint investigation systems helped lead to the development of the more aggressive strategies known as affirmative action. Affirmative action is intended to supplement earlier attempts to promote equal opportunity by requiring organizations to act in a positive fashion to curtail and overcome the effects of discrimination directed against groups such as minorities and women without waiting for individual complaints. Early efforts at affirmative action involved work force analysis, the removal of barriers to the placement of women and minorities, recruitment programs, and upward mobility training programs noted earlier. Numerical goals and timetables represent an additional step in the evolution of the concept of affirmative action. The establishment of goals and timetables forces the employer or institution of higher education to develop plans to respond to minority or female underrepresentation in their organizations.

Readers might ask, however, whether the use of goals and timetables, and their focus on encouraging the selection of minorities and women, contradicts the notion of *equality* of opportunity. Because goals and timetables imply that limited preferences may be given to minorities and women under certain circumstances, the policy clearly does not treat every person equally. In general, the argument for preferential forms of affirmative action is that to overcome the effects of past and current discrimination, ethnicity or sex must be taken into account. Advocates argue that goals must be set for the representation of minorities and women that reflect reasonable estimates of what their representation would have been if discrimination against them had not occurred in the first place.

The various approaches to affirmative action and equal opportunity policy in current practice are represented in Table 1.1. Individual-based policies such as complaint processing programs and early affirmative action in the form of recruitment or upward mobility programs comprise traditional equal opportunity efforts based on furthering the principle of nondiscrimination. Numerical-based preferential approaches to affirmative action supplement and transcend traditional strategies for achieving equal opportunity.

Table 1.1
AFFIRMATIVE ACTION AND EQUAL OPPORTUNITY.

Individual-Based "Reactive" Policies	Group-Based "Proactive" Policies (Affirmative Action)	
Approaches that Predate Affirmative Action	*Early Approaches to Affirmative Action*	*Preferential Approaches to Affirmative Action*
• Laws prohibiting discrimination • Procedures for the investigation and resolution of complaints	• Work force analysis • Removal of artificial barriers to minority and female selection • Career development and upward mobility programs • Recruitment and outreach efforts	• Voluntary goals and timetables for the selection of members of targeted groups • Consent decrees specifying selection goals and timetables • Court-ordered selection goals and timetables
Equal Employment Opportunity Programs Based on a Strict Interpretation of the Principle of Nondiscrimination	**Programs that Transcend Equality of Opportunity and Nondiscrimination in a Strict Sense by Permitting Preferences**	

Affirmative Action and the Distribution of Opportunity

The controversy over affirmative action is understood most clearly with the realization that such policies are intended to redistribute opportunity from those who have been historically advantaged (e.g., primarily white men) to those who have suffered disadvantages because of race, ethnicity, sex, or other traits or circumstances.[21] By their nature, many redistributive policies involve the transfer of resources from the "haves" to the "have nots."[22] In the context of affirmative action, these transfers involve highly valued jobs, coveted seats in educational institutions, and other opportunities that allow people to prosper and succeed. Because the stakes are high, the outcomes can be extremely important for people on both sides of the debate. Employment, for example, provides the means by which most individuals support themselves and their families financially. In addition, employment can be an avenue to self-fulfillment, a way of defining who one is and what one does. Also, the importance of educational attainment to career success can hardly be overstated. It is not surprising, therefore, that policies operating to alter the distribution of employment or educational opportunities will be opposed by some individuals from groups that have historically been advantaged relative to racial or ethnic minorities and women.[23] The erosion of nonminority and male advantage may be seen by some nonminority and men as unjustly detrimental to their prospects, but the extent to which their personal chances for employment or college admission actually decline in any specific instance is usually very small, particularly in the case of affirmative action programs targeting minorities.[24]

The forms of affirmative action that are most visibly redistributive and are most vulnerable to criticism are those involving the use of preferences for women or minorities because the existence of preferences contradicts the concept of pure equality of opportunity. Few people will oppose affirmative action efforts grounded firmly on the principle of nondiscrimination, such as broader recruitment or outreach programs, but they will contest preferential approaches (including goals and timetables), arguing that a strict interpretation of equal opportunity should prevail. From this point of view, preferences amount to what has been called "reverse discrimination" against nonminority males and sometimes nonminority women. This, no doubt, was the perception of Alan Bakke, a white male who wanted to become a medical student at the University of California at Davis in the 1970s, but who, as is widely known, was initially denied admission while minority students, who in Bakke's view were "less" qualified than he, were enrolled. Bakke sued the Regents of the University of California for reverse discrimination.[25] There was no question, however, that the minority students enrolled were qualified for admission and that their longing for a career in the medical profession was no less than that of Mr. Bakke. This is the agony of affirmative action. If we are to move away from a system in which nonminorities and especially nonminority men have historically been advantaged to a system where there is greater equality, opportunities must be redistributed. Chapter 5 of this book provides a review of the Bakke case and its outcome.

The Role of the Courts

Ultimately, of course, the judiciary plays an important part in sorting out conflict over affirmative action. More than a dozen affirmative action cases have been argued before the U.S. Supreme Court, and scores of other cases have been addressed by federal district and circuit courts of appeal. Attempts to synthesize judicial opinions regarding the legality of affirmative action programs are difficult, however, since it frequently appears that court decisions on the issue are disjointed and inconsistent. Thernstrom and Thernstrom have argued that "[a]nyone who looks for doctrinal consistency in the Supreme Court's decisions on employment discrimination will be severely disappointed."[26] A cursory review of decisions regarding preferential affirmative action could reinforce such an opinion. In those cases, the courts have at times upheld the legality of affirmative action and at other times they have struck it down, but because affirmative action comes in a variety of specific forms and must meet a range of legal requirements, divergent rulings on its legality hardly constitute doctrinal inconsistency.

The difficulty of interpreting court decisions on affirmative action occurs in part because different standards of review are applied when the courts assess the legality of the policy, and those standards vary based primarily on the nature of the legal challenge to affirmative action. For example, one can oppose affirmative action involving race or sex preferences in employment by arguing that it violates Title VII of the Civil Rights Act of 1964. Title VII is, of course, the federal statute that prohibits racial, ethnic, or sex discrimination in employment. The argument in such a claim would essentially be that affirmative action is a form of discrimination. The Supreme Court has ruled, however, that affirmative action that permits minority or female preferences will be allowed under Title VII if it conforms to certain specific limitations—including that the program must be designed to address a manifest racial or sex imbalance in the positions at issue, that it be a temporary measure designed to correct an imbalance rather than maintain a particular balance, and that qualifications of individuals be considered along with race or sex. In practice, those standards have not been particularly difficult to meet, and thus the statutory limitations imposed on affirmative action are not exceedingly onerous. In the two cases in which the Supreme Court has reviewed preferential affirmative action challenged under Title VII, the policy has been upheld.[27] As a result of those decisions, and because a statutory challenge under Title VII is the only mechanism by which an affirmative action program by a private employer may be opposed, the legal parameters for affirmative action in the context of private employment are not overly restrictive. Private employers, therefore, have some latitude in fashioning preferential affirmative action programs.

When affirmative action is undertaken by government organizations, however, the legal framework is different than that for the private sector. Government actions must comply with Title VII, as discussed above, but they must also conform to constitutional constraints. The Fifth and Fourteenth Amendments to the U.S. Constitution prohibit the federal government and the states (and local jurisdictions), respectively, from denying any individual equal protection of the laws.[28] When government draws distinctions between people that lead it to treat some people differently than others, a potential exists for the denial of equal protection. Certainly, government affirmative action programs that permit limited racial or sex-based preferences involve distinctions drawn in terms of race or sex, and, consequently, such programs may be challenged on the grounds that they violate the requirements of equal protection. A long history of jurisprudence abounds on issues of equal protection, but as the law now stands, the courts impose a rather restrictive standard of review on any programs that involve government distinctions along racial lines. That standard, known as "strict scrutiny," places the burden on government to show that the distinction serves a "compelling government interest" and is "narrowly tailored" to meet that interest. This burden has proved to be particularly difficult to meet; and when strict scrutiny is applied by the courts to government affirmative action programs, the result often has been that those programs are disallowed. As a consequence, the practical constraints imposed on government affirmative action (whether in employment, contracting, or higher education) are much more confining than those imposed on private employers. Added to this legal complexity is the fact that the specific form by which affirmative action preferences operate will also influence judicial outcomes. Efforts to displace nonminority employees, for example, to make room for minority workers are not tolerated.[29]

It is of further interest to note that until 1995, affirmative action programs implemented by the federal government were given greater constitutional tolerance than those of state or local governments. This particular additional distinction was largely what accounted for the Supreme Court's decision to uphold affirmative action in the form of minority business enterprise set-asides in *Fullilove v. Klutznick* (a federal program), to strike down set-asides in *Richmond v. Croson* (a municipal program), and then to uphold them again in *Metro Broadcasting v. FCC* (a federal program).[30] The Court reasoned that federal programs should be subjected to a less rigorous standard of constitutional review than strict scrutiny. Any misunderstanding that may have been caused by the distinction between federal and state (or local) government programs was effectively ended, however, in 1995 following the decision in *Adarand v. Pena,* where the Court ruled that the most restrictive constitutional/equal protection standard (i.e., strict scrutiny) must be applied to federal efforts just as it had been applied earlier to programs by states and local governments.[31] A full discussion of these and other cases is provided in chapters 5 and 6.

An apparent distinction also exists between the constitutional limitations imposed on affirmative action in the context of admissions to public institutions of higher education and affirmative action in public employment. In the summer of 2003, the Supreme Court ruled in *Grutter v. Bollinger* that student body diversity at the University of Michigan School of Law was a sufficiently compelling reason to justify the limited and flexible consideration of race or ethnicity in admissions procedures in public colleges or universities.[32] (This case is reviewed in more detail in chapter 6.) The Supreme Court has not found that diversity in the public employment context is similarly compelling. The circumstances necessary to uphold preferential affirmative action in that context are, as a result, much less clear.

The Objective of This Book

The development and application of affirmative action in the United States is a more complex issue than has often been acknowledged. The debate and confusion are not surprising given (1) the variety of meanings attached to the term; (2) the fact that affirmative action involves the highly charged issue of the distribution of employment, business, and educational opportunities; and (3) the complexity of court decisions on the subject. When speaking about "affirmative action," one could be referring to a number of different programs and interested individuals may be uncertain about what is required under a particular policy or when certain kinds of action are legally permissible. Managers and administrators who want to comply with the law may not always know what they can and cannot do.

Because affirmative action is controversial, the meanings of key concepts associated with it tend to be insufficiently addressed or sometimes misrepresented to better support particular lines of argument in the public debate. Even comments by well-intentioned observers are misleading at times, adding further to a general level of misunderstanding. CBS News political analyst Laura Ingraham, for example, argued on an evening broadcast in 1998 that "preferences have been struck down by most every single court in this country, including the Supreme Court, as unconstitutional."[33] Regarding the use of preferences, Ingraham suggested that "[i]t's unfair and it's unjust, and it's now unconstitutional."[34] Perhaps Ingraham may be forgiven for being caught up in a heated exchange, but to this date, no general finding by the Supreme Court states that preferences are uniformly unconstitutional. In fact, before Ingraham made her comment, the Court specified that in certain circumstances preferential policies may pass a constitutional test.[35] In *University of California v. Bakke*, the Court suggested that race could be considered in some instances as a factor in university admissions, and to do so, of course, implies that, "other things being equal," some preference will be given to minority applicants.[36] In other cases from the 1980s, the Court had indicated that evidence of past discrimination by an employer may provide a sufficient constitutional justification for preferential affirmative action policies, although the particular programs at issue in those cases were not upheld.[37] And, of course, in 2003 in *Grutter v. Bollinger*, as noted earlier, a majority of the Court affirmed the constitutionality of a preferential affirmative action program by the University of Michigan School of Law.[38] Furthermore, a focus on constitutionality neglects the fact that private organizations are not restricted by constitutional concerns for equal protection of the laws. Ingraham's comments clearly did not represent the full complexity of judicial rulings on affirmative action, but inattention to nuance and detail is not uncommon in debate over the policy, whether on television or elsewhere. The unfortunate result is more confusion than clarity.

The purpose of this book is to offer a review and analysis intended to raise an awareness of the history, the impact, and the legal parameters of affirmative action. The goal is not to adduce new arguments or novel interpretations but, rather, to synthesize and summarize existing information in such a way as to promote a fuller understanding of the issues involved. The past several years have seen significant developments substantially altering the nature of affirmative action programs. The legal parameters for preferential affirmative action have been more fully specified. As a result, a carefully constructed and comprehensive examination of affirmative action is now appropriate and desirable. By taking a broad view of programs in the public sector (i.e., programs implemented by federal, state, and local government organizations), as well as programs by private-sector organizations, the intention is to foster an appreciation of the complexity of the affirmative action debate. Hopefully, this analysis will be useful to individuals who want to know where affirmative action stands, how the policy ended up where it is, and where the policy might be going in the future.

The analysis in this work draws in part on historical institutionalism for theoretical grounding.[39] This perspective operates from an assumption that the development and implementation of equal employment opportunity and affirmative action policies have been significantly influenced by the nature and operation of our political institutions. Relations among the three branches of the federal government and the formal and informal rules and procedures governing their conduct, for example, have determined the shape of our responses to discrimination in fundamental ways. Institutional factors help us understand why the U.S. Congress was slow in reacting to discrimination and why for decades the government's response rested exclusively on presidential executive orders. A historical–institutional approach also provides insight into the development of case law regarding affirmative action that might not be obtained by use of other perspectives.

Within this framework, chapter 2 explains the historical development of equal employment opportunity policy, stressing the importance of federal executive orders and statutory law. Chapter 3 provides a full discussion of the development of preferential affirmative action and its implications for equal opportunity. Chapter 4 explores the rationale for affirmative action. The broad range of arguments for affirmative action are considered in this chapter, along with points made by those opposed to the policy. Among other issues, the relationship between affirmative action and justice shall be explored. The connection between affirmative action and civil society and the notion of representative bureaucracy, which has significant implications for affirmative action in the public sector, are also discussed. Chapters 5 and 6 outline the legal boundaries of affirmative action as defined by the courts. These chapters present an up-to-date review of Supreme Court decisions on the legality of affirmative action when it is challenged on either statutory or constitutional grounds. Included here is a detailed review of the landmark decision from 2003 in *Grutter v. Bollinger* and its companion case (*Gratz v. Bollinger*) from the University of Michigan.

The effects of affirmative action are the subject of chapter 7. No discussion of affirmative action would be complete without consideration of the influence of the policy on such issues as minority and female employment. Has affirmative action led to employment gains for targeted groups? What about affirmative action in higher education? What has its impact on campus been? How are we able to know the effects of affirmative action? What methodological issues must be addressed in our assessments? Is it possible that the symbolism associated with affirmative action as an effort to combat historical patterns of discrimination may be as important as actual changes in employment or other trends? These are among some of the important questions taken up in this chapter.

Finally, chapter 8 offers some brief concluding observations. Questions regarding the future of affirmative action are considered here. The last chapter of this book explores the issue of whether affirmative action will remain a significant force in years to come or whether our society will move beyond affirmative action in employment, government contracting, and higher education. Hopefully, the readers of this work will find the discussion informative and the arguments presented thoughtful and useful. Ultimately, the question is what shall be done to combat racial, ethnic, and sex discrimination, which has operated for centuries to suppress the advancement of minorities and women. The next chapter examines some of our earliest efforts to deal with this problem.

two

Early Efforts Focusing on Equality of Opportunity

The history of discrimination directed against minorities and women in the United States because of racist, ethnocentric, or sexist attitudes has been long and painful. Discrimination has bred violence, fear, and desperation and has left an indelible mark on the American psyche. It is based on the notion that some people, distinguished by their cultural identities or immutable characteristics such as sex or the amount of melanin present in the skin, are inferior to others. Such attitudes flourishing in a country whose founding documents eloquently embrace notions of equality are ironic and disappointing.[1] Writing in the mid-1940s, Gunnar Myrdal described the problem of race relations in the United States as one of the most urgent dilemmas facing American society.[2] Since the time of Myrdal's influential book, Americans have been struggling with the question of how to deal with discrimination most effectively. Not until the later decades of the twentieth century, however, were substantial efforts undertaken to address practices that kept untold numbers of women and minorities from achieving what their talents and abilities would allow. Affirmative action, in all of its various forms, is an outgrowth of those efforts.

This chapter examines major developments in the struggle to overcome the problem of discrimination against minorities and women and explores the emergence of the earliest affirmative action programs. As the discussion unfolds, two points become increasingly clear. The first is that responses to the problem of discrimination have evolved and expanded gradually over time. Successive layers have been added in attempts to devise more effective policies, with each succeeding strategy more vigorous than its predecessor. Growth in the strength of these efforts was undoubtedly necessary, but as programmatic efforts expanded, so too did the controversy.

The second point is that the variety of strategies that have been devised to deal with discrimination, and the evolution of those efforts, have been shaped in large part (as was suggested in the previous chapter) by the character of our governmental institutions, the rules by which those institutions operate, and the manner in which they have interacted. The membership of our legislative assemblies and the will of various political executives have profoundly influenced the quality of our policy responses to discrimination. Generally speaking, public officials warmed slowly to the idea that government should work to oppose historic patterns of inequity. In many instances, responses were as much the product of political machinations as they were the result of a commitment to justice.

Initial Efforts to Combat Discrimination: A Focus on Executive Authority

The earliest administrative programs designed to deal specifically with the problem of racial discrimination can be traced back only as far as the early 1940s.[3] Those initial efforts were to a significant degree a reaction to injustices suffered by African Americans as a result of employment practices in the private sector and in government. To fully appreciate the circumstances of the time, readers should recall that in the late 1930s, the nation was struggling to overcome the ravages of the Great Depression. The Roosevelt administration had created new federal agencies to respond to the economic crisis, and numerous public works projects were undertaken to create employment opportunities and to improve the nation's infrastructure. In addition, by the autumn of 1939 Europe and much of Asia were engulfed in war. The United States was appropriating large sums for national defense, and military contractors were consequently expanding operations and the size of their work forces. The new jobs that were created would benefit countless workers, but discriminatory practices excluded African Americans from most of those opportunities.

Nevertheless, government was hesitant to address the plight of black laborers. Federal decision makers found numerous problems confronting the nation that were more pressing than the issue of employment discrimination against African Americans. Politically, discrimination did not generate significant public attention. Many congressional leaders, especially conservative southern Democrats, were not predisposed to act on the matter. Still, two pieces of national legislation did pass containing limited provisions prohibiting discriminatory actions. The Hatch Act of 1939, whose main purpose was to restrict federal workers' political activities, provided that it would be unlawful to "deprive . . . any person of any employment . . . made possible by any Act of Congress appropriating funds for work relief or relief purposes, on account of race, creed, [or] color."[4] Similarly, legislation from 1940, designed to extend merit system coverage to several newly created federal agencies and to extend coverage of the classification Act of 1923, also prohibited discrimination on the basis of "race, creed, or color" in the federal service.[5] Shortly before passage of that legislation, President Roosevelt issued Executive Order 8587, which also prohibited racial discrimination in the federal service.[6] But as little was done to enforce the legislative provisions or the executive order, the policy of nondiscrimination was more a sentiment than a reality.

An actual program to deal with discrimination did not take shape until 1941. Frustrated with continuing employment discrimination in jobs funded by federal dollars, black leaders planned a mass march and rally on the Mall in Washington, D.C., to register black dissatisfaction. They were led by A. Philip Randolph, who had earlier founded the organization of African American railway workers known as the Brotherhood of Sleeping Car Porters. The protest was scheduled to occur on July 1, 1941.[7] Randolph successfully mobilized black leaders and organizations across the country and projected that as many as 100,000 people would attend. The march would be a dramatic and bold demonstration of African American anger with continued discrimination in defense industries and government employment. Randolph and the other leaders of the movement sought decisive action by the Roosevelt administration in the form of an executive order

prohibiting discrimination by federal agencies, the armed forces, and defense contractors.

President Roosevelt was, for a number of reasons, decidedly cool to the
idea. Politically, Roosevelt was in a tenuous position. If he came out forcefully in favor of the integration of blacks into the workplace, he risked
losing the support of key southern leaders and their constituents who
formed a major portion of the Democratic party coalition. Furthermore,
a mass protest rally by 100,000 angry blacks calling attention to racial injustice in the United States would be a significant embarrassment for the
administration.[8] Roosevelt had worked hard to unify Americans in the
face of an unprecedented national economic emergency and in opposition
to Nazi aggression in Europe. The march on Washington threatened to
expose racism in the United States just as we were confronting the possibility of war against fascism and racism in Germany. Roosevelt also feared
that violence would erupt during the Washington rally and that social
unrest would spread across the country and would possibly even disrupt
military discipline.[9]

In an attempt to appease Randolph and the other leaders of the march
on Washington movement, Roosevelt sent a letter to the co-chairmen of
the Office of Production Management restating the administration's opposition to discrimination. This fell far short of an effective response to discrimination, however, and the march organizers held their ground. The
president then sent Mayor Fiorello LaGuardia of New York and First Lady
Eleanor Roosevelt to try to dissuade Randolph and his colleagues, but as
noted by Samuel Krislov, the leaders of the march movement "persisted in
the face of pleas, threats, and cajolings."[10] The president had no recourse
but to try to accommodate the black leaders' demands. He met with Randolph and Walter White of the National Association for the Advancement
of Colored People on June 18, less than two weeks before the scheduled
march. A few days later, on June 25, Roosevelt issued Executive Order 8802
creating the President's Committee on Fair Employment Practice to receive and investigate complaints of discrimination in employment by defense contractors and federal departments and agencies.[11] The march on
Washington was canceled.

The president's executive order launched a new era with respect to the
federal government's concern with civil rights. As Merl Reed notes in his

insightful book on this development, the creation of the President's Committee on Fair Employment Practice represented "the first time since Reconstruction, [that] the nation had a federal agency devoted exclusively to minority problems."[12] Establishment of the committee officially associated the federal government with the struggle to end discrimination against racial minorities.[13] Funding for the committee's operation came from a presidential emergency fund included in the appropriation for the Executive Office of the President.[14] That procedure allowed the committee to operate without the direct congressional approval that would be required for a specific budgetary appropriation.

By the autumn of 1941, the president's committee, later known simply as the Fair Employment Practices Committee, or FEPC, had established procedures for receiving complaints of discrimination. The FEPC had authority to investigate these complaints and to make recommendations for their resolution, but it could not directly force employers to change employment practices. The committee was effective, nevertheless, in calling attention to the problem of discrimination by holding highly publicized, open hearings where charges of discrimination were aired. Through this strategy, the FEPC confronted "some of the largest and most important defense contractors in the country, questioned their employment practices, and exposed them to publicity."[15]

Within a few months, the committee had established a reputation as a serious force against employment discrimination. It heard complaints against federal government agencies in addition to those directed against defense contractors. But as the FEPC became more active, the agency's opponents became more vocal. Following a series of investigations of discriminatory practices by defense contractors in the south, and after an especially contentious hearing in Birmingham, Alabama, southern politicians mobilized themselves against the committee. The governor of Alabama, Frank Dixon, argued that the FEPC was threatening the entire southern social fabric by opposing racial segregation, which had been the foundation of southern social and economic life for generations.[16] Congressman John Rankin of Mississippi called for a congressional investigation into the committee's actions, and the influential senator from Georgia, Richard Russell, reportedly called the FEPC "the most dangerous force in existence in the United States."[17] In January of 1943, in part because of this kind of criticism, the White House intervened directly and ordered the FEPC to cancel a hearing on alleged discriminatory practices by southern railroads. Later that same year, Roosevelt issued a new executive order and reorganized the committee.[18] The president increased funding for the agency, and for the first time, the FEPC was able to establish field offices. But along with those changes came a reshuffling of the committee membership and the removal of the most ardent supporters of the agency's practices who were replaced by individuals the president believed would be less antagonistic.[19]

Still, the committee could not stand long against the relentless attacks from white conservative politicians. Early in 1944, Senator Russell of Georgia sponsored an amendment to the Independent Offices Appropriation Act of 1940 that was designed to prohibit the indirect funding of agencies as had occurred with the FEPC.[20] Under the Russell Amendment, which became law soon after its introduction, any agency that had operated for more than one year without a direct appropriation from Congress would be terminated. This meant that the FEPC had to seek congressional support. To the surprise of Russell and other southern segregationists, an appropriation nearly equal to the agency's request passed in the House of Representatives and the Senate by small margins that year.[21]

The following year the FEPC was decidedly less fortunate. Money was appropriated once more, but this time it was for only half of the previous year's funding level. Substantial cuts in the committee's operations were required.[22] A year later, Congress provided no appropriation and the committee officially ceased operation. During its lifetime, however, the FEPC successfully documented discrimination in several industries and government agencies. It inspired hope among civil rights leaders that further progress could be made, and it set a precedent for future civil rights initiatives based on the president's authority to act independently of Congress. Roosevelt used his executive authority to attack discrimination by setting the terms and conditions of federal contracts and by regulating the federal civil service. Both of those approaches were to become central avenues by which the government could achieve equal employment opportunity objectives.

Following the death of the FEPC, the government was left with no administrative mechanism to investigate discrimination by private employers. The nondiscrimination clause required in government contracts was by itself largely ineffective. The Civil Service Commission (CSC) assumed responsibility for ensuring equal opportunity in federal employment, but its disposition toward the pursuit of equal rights for minorities was suspect, and little progress was made.[23] Initially, President Truman sought fair employment legislation but opted for use once again of the executive order when it was clear that Congress could not be moved to take legislative action.[24]

In July of 1948, Truman issued Executive Order 9980, establishing a Fair Employment Board (FEB) within the CSC.[25] The FEB was charged with responsibility for receiving and investigating complaints of discrimination in federal employment much as the FEPC had done earlier, but only on appeal from departments and agencies following their attempts at adjudication. As Ruth P. Morgan points out, however, the FEB soon learned that the number of formal complaints filed could not be accepted as a true measure of the amount of discrimination in government.[26] Many minorities feared retaliation or retribution if they spoke out against discrimination. As a result, the FEB initiated a limited and experimental program of positive or constructive action in cooperation with federal departments and agencies. This program involved the establishment of contacts with minority organizations, efforts to encourage minority group members to apply for federal jobs, and improved training for lower-level workers.[27]

While the FEB was busy working for nondiscrimination in the federal civil service, the question of discrimination in private employment remained. As noted earlier, the ability to shape federal contract provisions was the major source of government influence over private employment practices. President Truman sought to revitalize the nondiscrimination clause required in government contracts by creating, through Executive Order 10308 in December 1951, the Committee on Government Contract Compliance.[28] This committee was given authority to receive and investigate complaints of discrimination levied against government contractors. Truman's model was the FEPC and thus his strategy was a bit risky given the ultimate fate of that agency. However, Congress had retreated from the principle embodied in the Russell Amendment by authorizing, in the Independent Offices Appropriation Act of 1946, the financing of "interdepartmental committees" through contributions from participating departments and agencies. This change in the law meant that administrative committees that served the common interests of multiple departments and agencies could be formed and funded indirectly from money appropriated to those departments and agencies.[29] Again, the president turned to this approach only after it was clear that fair employment practices legislation for the private sector, which he had repeatedly urged Congress to pass, would not be forthcoming.[30] Ultimately, however, the committee stirred little controversy since it was decidedly nonaggressive in its orientation. In fact, Morgan argues that the committee functioned largely as a "study group."[31]

Following Dwight D. Eisenhower's election in 1952, several members of Truman's Government Contract Compliance Committee resigned. The status of the committee remained uncertain until August 13, 1953 when, after Congress had adjourned, Eisenhower issued Executive Order 10479 replacing Truman's organization with a new Contract Compliance Committee. To elevate the status of the new committee, Eisenhower appointed the vice president, Richard M. Nixon, to serve as the committee's chairman. Eisenhower's order also strengthened the nondiscrimination clause provided in all government contracts by placing a positive burden on contractors to post notices at work sites acknowledging their agreement to provide employment without discrimination on the basis of race, color, national origin, or religion. Eisenhower's committee also stressed that nondiscrimination was required with respect to promotion, transfer, and other personnel actions in addition to hiring.[32] The committee assisted contracting agencies in the process of investigating complaints and obtaining compliance with the national policy of nondiscrimination. Any failure to come into compliance with the law could result in the loss of current and future contracts. Vice President Nixon urged contracting agencies to take such action when necessary, but the vice president's recommendation on that question was not often followed.[33]

In January 1955, the effort to ensure nondiscrimination in the federal civil service also received President Eisenhower's imprimatur with the issuance of Executive Order 10590.[34] Until that time, Truman's FEB had continued to operate within the CSC. But following a dispute between the FEB and the Department of the Treasury, Eisenhower abolished Truman's organization and created a new committee outside of the CSC. This organization was known as the President's Committee on Government Employment Policy (PCGEP). The PCGEP was to investigate complaints from federal employees, but like its predecessor, it was only authorized to advise agencies of its findings. The committee's success, therefore, was dependent upon the persuasive abilities of the committee membership.

Positive Responsibilities for Employers: An Active and Affirmative Orientation

In the 1960s a significant change occurred in efforts to combat discrimination. Early in his term, President John F. Kennedy announced his support for the concept of equal employment opportunity and immediately reorganized the federal effort. Executive Order 10925, issued on March 6, 1961, consolidated the government contract compliance and federal civil service programs under yet another newly established authority known as the President's Committee on Equal Employment Opportunity (PCEEO).[35] The Contract Compliance Committee and the PCGEP, established by Eisenhower, were dissolved. Vice President Lyndon B. Johnson was named chairman of the new committee. The secretary of labor was vice chairman with direct responsibility for implementing the work of the committee, which was funded from contributions from all federal departments and agencies subject to the committee's jurisdiction.[36]

The PCEEO received and investigated complaints as its predecessors had done earlier, but Kennedy's order required substantially more than a focus on complaint processing. By this time, it was clear that a program built largely on the investigation of complaints would work only to the extent that individuals were willing to bring allegations of discrimination to appropriate authorities, and minority group members in discriminatory or hostile environments often were not comfortable filing complaints. Furthermore, the registering of complaints would not, by itself, ensure that corrective action would be taken. The often subtle and elusive nature of discrimination made proving discriminatory practices difficult, and even when such a finding was reached, the government's record of securing satisfactory implementation of its recommendations for resolution was, up to this point in time, mixed at best. For these reasons Truman's FEB had suggested that much of the discrimination in the federal service went unreported. Eisenhower's PCGEP also noted the limitations of relying primarily on complaint investigation in the effort to enforce nondiscrimination policy. According to David H. Rosenbloom, the PCGEP "found that a complaint-oriented system was inherently of limited utility because there was 'no doubt that many' complaints were 'withheld because of reluctance' on the part of complainants 'to become identified as trouble makers or risk reprisal,' and because 'even with complaints at hand discrimination is often elusive and difficult to pin down.'"[37]

Kennedy responded to the growing perception that complaint processing by itself was ineffective by placing new obligations on employers. Under earlier programs, employers were directed *not to do* certain things. They were not to engage in discriminatory behavior that would disadvantage minority job applicants or employees because of race or ethnicity. Kennedy supplemented that approach by requiring employers *to take specific actions* to promote greater equality of opportunity. The difference, of course, is between a negative prohibition on one hand and an affirmative or positive requirement on the other. The shift in orientation was articulated in Part III of Kennedy's order, which outlined new obligations for federal contractors and subcontractors. Section 301 of Part III states in part that:

> [t]he contractor will not discriminate against any employee or applicant for employment because of race, creed, color, or national origin. The contractor will take *affirmative action* to ensure that all applicants are employed, and that employees are treated during employment, without regard to their race, creed, color, or national origin. Such action shall include, but not be limited to, the following: employment, upgrading, demotion or transfer; recruitment or recruitment advertising; layoff or termination; rates of pay or other forms of compensation; and selection for training, including apprenticeship. The contractor agrees to post in conspicuous places, available to employees and applicants for employment, notices to be provided by the contracting officer setting forth the requirements of this nondiscrimination clause (emphasis added).[38]

With respect to federal government employment, the order specified that:

[t]he President's Committee on Equal Employment Opportunity established by this order is directed immediately to scrutinize and study employment practices of the Government of the United States, and to consider and recommend additional *affirmative steps* which should be taken by executive departments and agencies to realize more fully the national policy of nondiscrimination within the executive branch of the Government (emphasis added).[39]

This policy orientation, which built on the earlier positive activities of the Truman and Eisenhower committees, meant that employers would be expected to take greater initiative in the battle against discrimination. Federal government agencies and private businesses with government contracts were expected to reach out to minority high school and college graduates and recruit them for employment. They were expected to offer training and apprentice programs to provide skills development that would enable minority applicants to qualify for entry-level and higher positions. Employers were expected to reevaluate qualifications standards to make certain that they were job related and did not artificially block the hiring or advancement of minorities who may not have enjoyed educational opportunities equivalent to those of majority whites. These activities, which were quite distinct from what had occurred earlier, represented the beginning of programmatic efforts known as affirmative action.

To help secure compliance with the order, the PCEEO required that government contractors file periodic compliance reports. The committee was authorized to levy sanctions against contractors who failed to comply by terminating their contracts, excluding them from future contracts, and requesting prosecution by the Department of Justice for contract violations.[40] The emphasis, however, was on encouraging employers to make good-faith efforts to fulfill the provisions of the order. Similar expectations were set for federal agencies, and in addition, the committee initiated an annual census of minority employment within the federal government.[41] During the Kennedy years, African American representation in the federal service rose to 13.1 percent, but they were almost exclusively in lower-level positions.[42] As a result, concern soon shifted to the problem of providing opportunities for minority employees to advance to middle- and higher-level positions in the federal service.[43]

When Lyndon Johnson ascended to the presidency, he initially maintained the PCEEO. Passage of the Civil Rights Act of 1964, however, brought
major changes in federal equal employment opportunity policy. Title VI of
the civil rights law prohibited discrimination by any organization receiving federal funds, including federal contractors, and Title VII directly prohibited discrimination by private employers, labor organizations, and employment agencies. Title VII also established a permanent agency, the Equal
Employment Opportunity Commission (EEOC), to supervise implementation of the policy of nondiscrimination and to receive, investigate, and
recommend resolutions of discrimination complaints. Thus, for the first
time a statutorily authorized agency was established specifically to combat
employment discrimination.

The provisions of the 1964 Civil Rights Act added a new dimension to
the government's equal employment opportunity enforcement process.
To a considerable extent, the mission of the PCEEO, as it related to private
employment, overlapped that of the newly created EEOC. The president's
committee regulated the employment affairs of government contractors.
The EEOC had authority over private employers whether they held government contracts or not. Politically conservative southern Democrats in
Congress sought to use the existence of the EEOC as an argument to abol-
ish the president's committee.[44] The PCEEO had implemented a relatively
aggressive program that required positive efforts by federal contractors to
overcome historical patterns of discrimination against minorities. Segregationists in Congress apparently preferred the new and relatively weak
EEOC to the more aggressive president's committee.[45] The Civil Rights Act
did not require the EEOC to establish a positive program of affirmative action. It was primarily an investigatory unit that would react to official complaints of discrimination. Senator Willis Robertson of Virginia, who served
on the Senate Appropriations Committee, led the attack on the PCEEO by
pushing for cuts from the budgets of agencies and departments equal to
their contributions to the president's committee. As an "inter-departmen-
tal committee," the PCEEO was dependent on support from the eighteen
agencies and departments who were subject to its jurisdiction. This placed
Johnson in an untenable position. If the president forced the agencies and
departments to contribute to the committee despite the cuts, their operating budgets would be substantially reduced.[46] Yet, if the president did not

require the contributions, the committee could not operate and affirmative action would be lost.

The president responded with Executive Order 11246 in September of 1965.[47] The order abolished the PCEEO, but transferred its responsibility for federal contract compliance to the Department of Labor. Oversight of the government's internal equal employment opportunity effort was transferred to the CSC, whose chairman, John Macy, was reportedly eager to establish an aggressive new program.[48] Importantly, Johnson's order maintained the affirmative action requirements imposed on federal contractors by President Kennedy and the similar positive emphasis required within federal departments and agencies.

Consequently, by the mid-1960s, affirmative action was a principle aspect of federal EEO policy with respect to contractors and the federal civil service. Some evidence suggests that, at least in certain instances, the effort, which included minority recruitment and outreach programs, was pursued vigorously. The Labor Department's own internal effort provides a good example. Representatives from the department visited numerous college campuses with noticeable minority enrollments in an attempt to encourage minority applicants.[49] Efforts were also made to contact minority organizations, to advertise job opportunities in minority media, and to develop upward mobility programs that would provide lower-level employees with access to higher-level positions. Additionally, with the issuance of Executive Order 11375 in October of 1967, women were for the first time also targeted for similar equal employment opportunity policy requirements.[50] Data on the federal employment of women were collected and published, along with data on minority employment, so that progress could be monitored.[51]

Conclusion

The development of equal employment opportunity policy illustrates well how the character of our political institutions helps to shape the formation of policy initiatives. The institutionally based political circumstances surrounding the establishment of President Roosevelt's FEPC provide a case in point. Even if Roosevelt had wanted to aggressively pursue an antidiscrimination policy, the fact that key positions in Congress were in the hands of segregationist southern Democrats—whose support Roosevelt needed for other political objectives—meant that the president could only proceed very cautiously. Certainly, no legislative initiatives would be introduced. As a result, Roosevelt resisted taking any action for as long as possible. He finally issued Executive Order 8802 only after African American civil rights leaders threatened to assemble tens of thousands of people in Washington to protest discrimination. Had it not been for the efforts of A. Philip Randolph and his associates, Roosevelt, most likely, would not have acted in any substantive way on this issue.

The indirect mechanism for funding Roosevelt's FEPC and the rather limited powers given the agency also clearly reflect the reality of institutional politics at the time. Direct appropriations for the FEPC were extremely problematic. In addition, it was unimaginable that the FEPC would be given the ability to force employers to abandon discriminatory practices.

Truman's struggles with Congress over similar issues provide further evidence of the importance of institutional dynamics. Indeed, given the political situation that Truman encountered, anything that was accomplished on civil rights during the late 1940s is surprising. The president worked hard for fair employment legislation, but after it was clear that Congress still would not act, he too turned to the executive order. Further, Truman placed primary emphasis on combating discrimination in the federal civil service—an area for which the constitution and earlier legislation established substantial presidential authority. As was previously discussed, Truman was much slower in dealing with the issue of discrimination by private contractors.

Finally, the struggle over early approaches known as affirmative action also gives insight into the manner in which institutional forces can place considerable constraints on policy options. As was noted, the PCEEO, established by President Kennedy, had developed what was considered to be an extremely aggressive program. The effort involved recruitment and outreach directed at the minority community. Within the federal civil service were upward mobility programs for lower-level employees and annual surveys to document progress in minority employment. Because these undertakings were much more vigorous than anything that had been implemented previously, the PCEEO quickly fell into disfavor with influential members of Congress who were opposed to substantial progress on matters of civil rights. When, despite the views of such people, the Civil Rights Act of 1964 became law, these same individuals worked more vigorously than ever for termination of the president's committee. The affirmative action program that the committee linked to federal contracts was not required under the Civil Rights Act, and at that time the act did not cover the federal civil service at all.[52] Thus, the attack on the president's committee could be seen primarily as an effort to kill affirmative action. Johnson's decision to split the committee's work and transfer it to the Department of Labor and the CSC by Executive Order 11246 was the only practical way for the president to save the affirmative action program. The less than parsimonious nature of the organization of responsibility for equal employment opportunity and affirmative action within the federal administrative structure that resulted from Johnson's action (and that largely remains in place to this day) was a product, in part, of the political and institutional exigencies of the early and mid-1960s.

The next chapter examines the further development of affirmative action in the late 1960s and beyond. The political context within which equal opportunity programs operated changed markedly as a result of the tumult of the 1960s and the effects of the civil rights and women's movements. That change led to the further development of affirmative action. During that time numerical goals for the selection of minorities (and women) and the preferences associated with those goals first emerged.

three

Affirmative Action and Preferential Selection

The decade of the 1960s was a significant period for the development of affirmative action, just as it was for social policy on a number of other important issues. By the end of the 1960s, a process was firmly in place that would dramatically transform affirmative action from an orientation grounded squarely on the principle of nondiscrimination in a literal sense to an approach that transcended a strict interpretation of the meaning of nondiscrimination. This transformation was accomplished largely through the use of numerical goals or targets for minority (and eventually female) employment and the limited preferences associated with those goals. Events that led to this significant shift had their roots in the social turmoil of the 1960s and the slow rate of progress achieved in the struggle to provide opportunities for racial minorities and women. The process of change began, however, only after the issuance of President Johnson's Executive Order 11246.

After the Department of Labor received responsibility for equal employment opportunity oversight with respect to government contractors as required by Johnson's order, Secretary of Labor Willard Wirtz established an enforcement agency within the department known as the Office of Federal Contract Compliance Programs (OFCCP).[1] This new office soon began to focus attention on the construction industry. The construction trades and the unions that organized them were notorious for discriminatory behavior. Minority workers were excluded from federally assisted apprenticeship programs and were denied job referrals from union hiring halls. At the same time, the nation was enjoying a building boom financed in part by a substantial influx of federal dollars. Indeed, as Hugh Davis Graham has pointed out, "by the late 1960s, federal funds were reaching 225,000 contractors involved in $30 billion in annual construction. This gave the federal government a direct economic impact on 20 million workers."[2]

The OFCCP organized its enforcement work around metropolitan labor markets, and rather than basing its strategy simply on a review of complaints, the office put into place a system of "pre-award" reviews of equal employment opportunity compliance pledged by organizations bidding for federal construction contracts. Although this process was slow to get underway, it was in place by 1967 when a contractor in Cleveland sought competitive advantage during pre-award negotiations by providing, along with a bid on work to be performed for the National Aeronautics and Space Administration, a list or "manning table" specifying the numbers of minority workers to be hired in various job categories if the firm received the government contract. The OFCCP embraced this concept as a demonstration of substantial commitment to the concept of providing opportunity to workers who had historically been excluded, and the agency helped the organization to secure the contract.[3]

The Philadelphia Plan: Introducing Numerical Goals

Following this experience, the OFCCP decided to require the development of minority employment goals by construction contractors in the city of Philadelphia because the civil rights records of those firms were so dismal. The construction companies blamed the trades unions with whom they worked for their poor record of minority employment. Segregation was the norm for construction and trades unions, and white unions, which tended to supply workers for the larger government-funded projects, were openly discriminatory in their attitudes. The construction firms found it necessary, nevertheless, to work with those unions and entered into agreements with them to hire only from union hiring halls.

The use of union hiring halls was a long-standing tradition and practice within the construction and buildings trades due to the project-focused nature of work in that industry. The hiring hall was a union-operated job referral center through which jobs would be distributed to workers. Because construction firms moved from one project to another, and each project varied in scope and in time to completion, firms could not maintain permanent employment rosters of skilled trades workers. Instead, they hired employees as needed for individual projects, and the union hiring hall acted under these circumstances as an employment agency referring employees to the firms. In that capacity, the unions met both the employees' need for a method of finding work and the employers' need for an efficient way to locate skilled workers. Union interests were also served since they were able to promote and protect the concerns of their members. Under these systems, union membership was a necessary condition for employment, which meant that the industry operated within a closed-shop arrangement, and white unions would not allow blacks to become members. In 1947, the Taft-Hartley Act prohibited the closed shop, but in subsequent years, the National Labor Relations Board found that enforcing such prohibition within the construction and building trades was difficult.[4]

Because of these difficulties, an amendment was added to the Labor-Management Reporting and Disclosure Act of 1959 (also known as the Landrum-Griffin Act) that attempted to set more realistic rules for the construction industry. That amendment is found in Section 705 of the law and provided, among other things, that:

> It shall not be an unlawful labor practice . . . for an employer engaged primarily in the building and construction industry to make an agreement . . . with a labor organization . . . because . . . such agreement . . . gives such labor organization an opportunity to refer qualified applicants for such employment.[5]

The law did not require these agreements; it merely permitted them. In addition, if such agreements were negotiated, unions would be free under the law to refer nonunion workers for available jobs, but as a practical matter, such referrals were not likely since they were not in the interest of the unions or union members. In short, Section 705 of the Landrum-Griffin Act sanctioned the operation of union hiring halls, and while they did not in a formal sense require union membership as a condition of employment, agreements establishing union referral systems had the effect of establishing closed-shop arrangements. As a practical result, employees selected by construction firms had to be union members before they could be hired, and, as previously noted, the white unions excluded black workers.

The OFCCP believed that the most effective way to deal with this situation was to place civil rights requirements on the firms bidding on federal contracts. Acting under guidance from the OFCCP, top officials from federal agency field offices in the Philadelphia metropolitan area established goals or objectives for minority employment by federal contractors. The OFCCP required contractors to agree to work toward meeting those goals. This process often meant that "contracts would be held up until bidders submitted detailed manning tables that listed by trade in all phases of the work the specific number of minority workers they pledged to hire."[6] The contractors' obligations were limited only by the availability of qualified minority laborers. Subsequently, this new approach focusing on numerical goals for minority employment as a way of dealing with discrimination in the construction trades became known as the Philadelphia Plan.

As might be expected, the Philadelphia Plan roused considerable opposition, but the chief opponent of the plan turned out to be the Comptroller General of the United States, Elmer Staats. As head of the government's General Accounting Office (GAO), Staats sought to protect his perception of the integrity of the government contracting process. The GAO (now known as the Government Accountability Office) is an arm of Congress charged with the task of auditing government programs to ensure compliance with statutory authority. Staats argued that no statutory basis existed for the Labor Department's new equal employment opportunity requirements for contractors contained in the Philadelphia Plan. The view from the GAO was that the plan was potentially inconsistent with the notion that contracts should always go to the lowest qualified bidder. Under the Philadelphia Plan, the pre-award review meant that negotiations over equal employment opportunity matters would take place with the apparent low bidder prior to the granting of the contract.[7] In the face of substantial GAO and congressional opposition, the Johnson administration, which by 1968 was preoccupied with numerous other domestic and international concerns, eventually abandoned this controversial approach to equal employment opportunity enforcement.

To the surprise of many proponents of affirmative action, however, the Nixon Administration revived the approach. Richard Nixon had chaired President Eisenhower's Government Contract Committee in the 1950s. Nixon's Secretary of Labor, George P. Schultz, became an advocate for the OFCCP and the specific approach to enforcement embodied in the Philadelphia Plan, and in the early summer of 1969, a revised plan was announced in a public ceremony in the city of Philadelphia. The major change from the Johnson years was that the new plan included minority employment goals specified by the OFCCP in the form of a range of percentages for minority representation. The goals, which were tied to estimates of the size of the minority labor market, were included with invitations for bids on federal contracts.[8] Why did the Nixon administration support affirmative action in this form? Perhaps Schultz was motivated by "personal convictions about the social irresponsibility of the construction-trades unions and the economic irrationality of racism in the American political economy," and President Nixon may well have shared those views.[9] Some observers have speculated, however, that the program's division of two influential and traditional Democratic party constituencies, African Americans and organized labor, was not unappreciated by the Republican administration.[10]

Opposition from the comptroller general continued, but the Nixon administration managed to weather the storm through the coordinated efforts of the president, the secretary of labor, and Attorney General John Mitchell. Eventually, congressional hearings were held in the fall of 1969 on two bills: one that would suspend President Johnson's Executive Order 11246 and make the Civil Rights Act of 1964 the sole legal basis for nondiscrimination policy, and another that would give final authority over the approval of federal contracts to the GAO. Neither bill gained substantial congressional support, however, and thus President Nixon and Secretary Schultz were able to achieve an important political victory.[11] Indeed, the congressional refusal to move decisively against the Philadelphia Plan when the opportunity was presented has been interpreted by many as an implicit legislative endorsement of the plan. A federal district judge dismissed a lawsuit filed against the Philadelphia Plan in March of 1970.[12]

Later that year, the Nixon administration, through Revised Order No. 4, extended the program to all activities of *all* major federal contractors.[13] In addition, in May of 1971, the chairman of the U.S. Civil Service Commission (CSC) endorsed the establishment of goals and timetables for minority employment as part of the affirmative action planning process by federal executive agencies.[14]

As a result of these developments, affirmative action soon became associated almost exclusively with the concept of goals and timetables for the employment of minorities and women. Advocates of this more aggressive approach to affirmative action were motivated in part by a perception that progress under earlier approaches had been too slow. It is useful to keep in mind the social context of the late 1960s that gave rise to this policy change. Urban unrest and rioting in the largely black ghettos in many metropolitan areas had risen to unprecedented levels. Numerous cities burned in the summers from 1964 to 1968. In the African American community, a growing sense of black nationalism developed, along with the belief that more vigorous movement from simple equality of opportunity to equality of results was necessary. This context provided a background against which equal employment opportunity policy was viewed. Discrimination had been shown to be very difficult to overcome. A consensus gradually emerged on the idea that efforts to provide opportunity for those who had been victimized by discrimination should be redoubled.

Numerical goals and timetables for minority and female employment were consistent with this view in that they placed an increased positive burden on employers. In effect, as noted earlier, goals and timetables for minority and female employment were an adaptation of the established management practice of responding to a problem by setting an objective and planning for its attainment.[15] But the focus on numerical goals creates a paradox in the enforcement of equal opportunity policy. The effort is based on the realization that the number of minority or female employees is often less than it presumably would have been had there been no discrimination directed against those groups. To ensure enforcement of civil rights with respect to equal opportunity, data on the numbers of minorities or women employed are necessary, and the implication is that when the numbers are too low, corrective action is needed. From this point, a logical step is to extend limited preferences to qualified women or members of minority groups to alter patterns of underutilization of those individuals. However, the notion of strict equality, or nondiscrimination, runs counter to such preferences. This is the dilemma that confronts policy makers and that is the basis for much of the conflict over affirmative action.

Further Developments in the 1970s:
The Growth of Preferential Programs

As the 1970s progressed, affirmative action policy continued to develop on the foundation laid during the Johnson and Nixon years. With respect to government employment, the need to base equal employment opportunity policy regarding the federal civil service on presidential orders finally ended with passage of the 1972 Equal Employment Opportunity Act.[16] This law amended the 1964 Civil Rights Act by expanding restrictions on discrimination in the private sector and prohibiting discrimination by state and local governments and in federal departments and agencies. Executive Order 11246 remained in effect, however, and the OFCCP continued its operations. The 1972 law also permitted the CSC to continue its responsibilities regarding the federal equal employment opportunity program.

Despite these efforts, progress remained slow. Though the 1972 Equal Employment Opportunity Act reaffirmed the federal affirmative action program implemented by the CSC, the employment of minorities and women in the upper grades of the federal service was persistently low. President Jimmy Carter, who strongly supported affirmative action, transferred federal equal employment opportunity responsibility to the Equal Employment Opportunity Commission (EEOC) under a reorganization order coinciding with the 1978 Civil Service Reform Act.[17] The 1978 act itself endorsed the idea of a representative bureaucracy (calling for "a work force reflective of the Nation's diversity"), established a new equal employment opportunity recruitment program for the federal civil service, and mandated that achievement of affirmative action goals would be one basis for evaluating the performance of members of the new Senior Executive Service.[18] For its part, the EEOC placed greater emphasis on numerical goals and timetables in agency affirmative action plans. Detailed instructions were developed for determining minority and female underrepresentation in higher-level positions, and goals and timetables were *required* when underrepresentation was documented. However, during the Reagan years, the EEOC backed away from this approach; regulations issued in 1987 permitted but no longer required agencies to utilize numerical goals.[19]

During the 1970s, many state and local governments also began to implement relatively aggressive affirmative action programs, but just a few years earlier, state and local jurisdictions were generally not heavily involved in this area. In fact, a 1967 Commission on Civil Rights survey found pervasive discrimination against minorities in state and local government employment.[20] Minority employees held mainly lower level blue-collar positions as common laborers in many jurisdictions, and particularly in the South, certain jobs were considered appropriate only for minorities.

In the 1960s, the only significant equal employment opportunity requirements imposed on the states, beyond the Fourteenth Amendment's guarantee of equal protection of the laws, were contained in federal standards requiring merit systems of employment in state programs receiving federal financial assistance and in Housing and Urban Development (HUD) programs administered by local government development agencies.[21] The merit system standards, developed originally in 1939, required selection, promotion, and compensation practices based on merit principles in agencies receiving federal funds. Discrimination on the grounds of religious or political opinion or affiliation was prohibited. A prohibition on racial discrimination was added in 1963. That same year, HUD required local development authorities "to take affirmative action to ensure that applicants are employed and employees are treated during employment, without regard to race, creed, color, or national origin."[22] But according to the Commission on Civil Rights, these programs had little effect on state and local employment.

In 1972, federal requirements on the states were considerably expanded. As noted, the 1972 Equal Employment Opportunity Act placed state and local governments (as well as the federal service) under the nondiscrimination provisions of Title VII of the Civil Rights Act of 1964. The 1972 legislation gave the EEOC the responsibility for supervising state and local employment practices and, perhaps most importantly, authorized legal action against government units charged with discrimination. State and local governments were required to adopt affirmative action programs and were to collect and report data on minority and female employment. By the mid-1970s, goals and timetables and the preferences they imply were firmly established as part of the affirmative action process.

The *Griggs* Case and Its Legacy:
The Concept of Disparate Impact

Another highly significant development occurred in the early 1970s, making the possibility of legal action by minority (or female) plaintiffs who alleged discrimination a more significant concern for a number of employers. This event was the 1971 decision by the U.S. Supreme Court in the case *Griggs v. Duke Power Company.*[23] The issue before the Court in this case was whether certain employment practices (specifically certain selection procedures) at the company's Dan River power-generating facility in Draper, North Carolina, were in violation of Title VII of the Civil Rights Act of 1964. The action was brought by Willie S. Griggs and twelve other black employees at the facility who alleged that employment and promotion requirements of the company impermissibly limited opportunities for black job applicants and employees. Title VII proscribed employment practices that intentionally drew distinctions between people along racial lines, but in this case the practices in question were applied equally to both blacks and whites though the outcome was different.

The situation is best understood by first realizing that the Dan River facility was organized into five separate operating departments consisting of labor, coal handling, operations, maintenance, and laboratory and test. The highest paying jobs in the labor department paid less than any of the jobs in any of the other departments. Prior to the effective date of the Civil Rights Act of 1964 (July 2, 1965), the company openly discriminated on the basis of race in its employment practices by permitting blacks to work only in the labor department. Additionally, since 1955, the company had a policy of requiring a high school diploma for *initial employment* (which was restricted to white applicants) in coal handling and the other higher-level departments and for *promotion* from coal handling to the other higher departments (operations, maintenance, or laboratory and test).

On July 2, 1965, as Title VII became effective, the company abandoned its openly discriminatory practices. Blacks would no longer be formally restricted to the labor department, but a high school diploma was made a prerequisite for *transfer* from labor to any other department. On that same day, the company also added a new requirement for *initial employment* in any department other than labor, mandating that applicants have satisfactory scores on two professionally prepared aptitude tests. Thus, any person (white or black) seeking initial employment in coal handling, operations, maintenance, or laboratory and test would need, after this date, a high school diploma *and* satisfactory test scores on the required tests. A high school diploma alone would make employees in the labor department eligible for promotion to positions in the other departments, but beginning in September of 1965, the company began to allow employees without a high school education to be promoted from labor to other departments provided they passed the two tests—the Wonderlick Personnel Test, which was supposed to measure general intelligence, and the Bennett Mechanical Comprehension Test. Neither test, however, provided a measure of ability to successfully perform or to learn to perform any job or category of jobs at the facility. The requisite scores used for both initial hiring and transfer were sufficiently high that they screened out approximately half of all high school graduates, and, consequently, the tests provided a more stringent standard than the high school graduation requirement. Both the high school requirement and the tests operated to exclude a substantially disproportionate number of blacks as compared to whites. Not until after charges had been filed in this case with the EEOC was a black employee (who happened to have a high school diploma) promoted from labor to coal handling. Nevertheless, the District Court and the Court of Appeals both found that Title VII had not been violated.

In a unanimous ruling, the Supreme Court reversed the decision of the Court of Appeals. The high court reasoned that under Title VII, "practices, procedures, or tests neutral on their face and even neutral in terms of intent, cannot be maintained if they operate to 'freeze' the status quo of prior discriminatory practices." The Court continued, arguing that Title VII "proscribes not only overt discrimination but also practices that are fair in form, but discriminatory in operation. The touchstone is business necessity. If an employment practice which operates to exclude Negros cannot be shown to be related to job performance, the practice is prohibited." In addition, the Court concluded that "good intent or the absence of discriminatory intent does not redeem employment procedures or testing mechanisms that operate as 'built-in headwinds'" for minority groups and are unrelated to measuring job capability.

The implications of this decision are profound. Following the Court's ruling in this case, Title VII not only prohibited overt or intentional discrimination, but it also prohibited discriminatory acts that were unintentional. The concept of unintentional discrimination was elaborated by the Court in subsequent decisions and eventually became known as disparate impact.[24] Under this doctrine, employment practices that appear nondiscriminatory and that are nondiscriminatory in intent may still be in violation of Title VII if they have the effect of disproportionately screening out applicants or employees along the lines of race, ethnicity, or sex. The burden of proof in such cases rests initially with employees, who believe they may have been victims of discrimination, to make out a *prima facie* case against their employer. Evidence of a *prima facie* case of discrimination may be derived from statistics that show a substantially lower rate of selection for members of any particular group compared to the selection rate of the group with the highest representation in the organization. Eventually, the *Uniform Guidelines on Employee Selection Procedures* issued jointly in 1978 by the Departments of Justice and Labor, the EEOC, and the CSC (now the Office of Personnel Management) settled on what became known as the four-fifths rule. This rule stated that a selection rate for a given group of less than 80 percent of the selection rate of the group whose members were selected most frequently would constitute *prima facie* evidence of discrimination.[25] Similarly, plaintiffs may also make a *prima facie* claim of discrimination by showing, again with the proper statistical evidence, that their level of employment in an organization is substantially less than the proportion of the qualified labor market consisting of members of their group.

After a *prima facie* case against an employer has been made, the burden shifts to the employer to defend the practices that produced any demonstrated statistical disparity by showing that those practices served a business necessity. Evidence that a selection examination is a valid predictor of ability to perform the particular job at issue would, for example, meet that burden. If the employer is successful in demonstrating business necessity, the employer is not in violation of Title VII, unless the employees can show that the employer's defense is a pretext for discrimination because other less discriminatory practices that also serve the identified business practices exist and can be utilized.

One way that an employer may be shielded from claims of discrimination under disparate impact theory (or claims of intentional discrimination as well for that matter) is if the employer's work force is sufficiently integrated to make any claim of statistical disparity along racial, ethnic, or gender lines impossible. Consequently, the ruling in the *Griggs* case, and the subsequent development of disparate impact theory, provided employers with an incentive to engage in employment practices, including affirmative action in its various forms, that would help to ensure minorities and women were not denied opportunity. For some employers, including state and local governments and institutions of higher education receiving federal financial assistance, the incentive may have been particularly salient since they would stand to lose federal assistance if found in violation of Title VII.

The *Ward's Cove* Decision: Attacking Disparate Impact Analysis

The state of the law regarding the concept of disparate impact, which had been settled for eighteen years and had been incorporated into the *Uniform Guidelines on Employee Selection Procedures,* was literally turned on its head by the Supreme Court in the June 5, 1989, decision in *Ward's Cove Packing Company v. Atonio.*[26] In that case, minority employees of two companies operating salmon canneries in Alaska filed a federal lawsuit alleging discrimination. The plaintiffs argued that minorities were employed almost exclusively in low-paying unskilled cannery jobs that involved cleaning and processing salmon, while other higher-paying jobs were reserved for nonminority personnel.

The Supreme Court rejected the plaintiffs' claim, noting that a comparison of the percentage of cannery workers in low-paying jobs who are minorities to the percentage of workers in higher-paying jobs who are minorities does not establish a *prima facie* case of disparate impact. The proper comparison, according to the Court, would be between the representation of minorities in the contested higher-paying jobs and the proportion of minorities in the relevant labor market with skills requisite for such jobs.

That point alone did not engender significant controversy, but the Court reached further in its decision, effectively refuting the principles laid down in the unanimous decision in *Griggs* and the progeny of that decision. The Court stated that after an appropriate statistical comparison had been made to establish *prima facie* evidence of discrimination, the plaintiffs would have to identify the clearly delineated specific employment practices responsible for creating the observed statistical disparity. Once that burden is met by the plaintiff, the employer could defend challenged practices by demonstrating that it serves a legitimate business purpose, but contrary to previous interpretations, the employer need not prove that a business purpose is served by the contested practices. Justice White, writing for the majority, argued that the burden of proof remains with employees at all times to demonstrate that challenged employment practices are selected precisely because of their discriminatory effect. According to Justice White, in a disparate impact case the employee "must prove that it was 'because of such individual's race, color,' etc. that he was denied a desired employment opportunity."[27]

After this decision minority plaintiffs had significantly more difficulty prevailing in Title VII discrimination cases because, in effect, they had to demonstrate that their employers intended to discriminate. Previously, as the dissenting justices in *Ward's Cove* noted, intent had no place in disparate impact analysis.[28] Disparate impact was considered to have occurred when personnel procedures that were neutral on their face and neutral in intent had a discriminatory impact, and no business justification for those procedures was apparent. This notion was articulated in *Griggs*, but following the decision in *Ward's Cove*, the distinction between disparate impact and disparate treatment (i.e., intentional discrimination) turned solely on the issue of whether the procedure was facially neutral. Evidence of intent to discriminate became necessary in both types of cases. Justice Stevens in his dissenting opinion noted that the majority in *Ward's Cove* acknowledged that under the *Griggs* decision an employment practice may be considered in violation of Title VII without evidence of the employer's intent to discriminate, but then, as Stevens argues, the majority "depart[ed] from the body of law engendered by this disparate impact theory, reformulating the order of proof and the weight of the parties' burdens."[29]

The Civil Rights Act of 1991 and
the Restoration of Disparate Impact Theory

The decision in *Ward's Cove* caused considerable concern among people interested in promoting efforts to overcome discrimination in employment. Because the decision rested on an interpretation of statutory law (Title VII), Congress could respond if a majority in both houses believed the Court had erred. Legislation could be passed revising the relevant statute to make explicit within the law the principles associated with disparate impact that had evolved from *Griggs*. That is precisely what Congress did when it passed civil rights legislation in 1990, which had the effect of amending the state of the law produced by the outcomes of, not only *Ward's Cove*, but several other cases decided in 1989 as well. As noted in chapter 1, George H.W. Bush (U.S. president from 1989 to 1993) promptly vetoed that legislation, calling it a "quota bill."[30] The following year, Congress passed similar legislation that incorporated the standards set out by *Griggs* directly into Title VII, but this time Bush signed the Act, known as the Civil Rights Act of 1991, into law.[31] As a result, the notion of disparate impact that had prevailed from 1971 to 1989 was restored. Minority plaintiffs were once again able to prevail in discrimination cases even though they might not prove intent, and so this significant incentive for employers to achieve a fair measure of diversity in their work forces was reestablished.

Eleventh Amendment Cases and Their Implications

In the mid- to late 1990s, however, in a series of cases regarding judicial enforcement of federal law with respect to the states, the Supreme Court limited congressional authority to regulate state employment practices. In a decision in 1996, for example, the Supreme Court ruled in *Seminole Tribe v. Florida* that Congress does not have the power under the commerce clause of Article I of the Constitution to abrogate a state's sovereign immunity in federal court.[32] In other words, state governments cannot be sued in federal court for a failure to implement provisions of federal law enacted pursuant to the authority of Congress contained in the commerce clause.[33] The Supreme Court's decision in this case rested on its interpretation of the

Constitution's Eleventh Amendment, which was designed to limit judicial authority relative to the states. In 1999, in *Alden et al. v. Maine,* the Court ruled that Congress also lacks the power, under Article I, to abrogate a state's sovereign immunity in state court.[34] This ruling, which is based on the same reasoning as *Seminole,* has the effect of preventing state employees from suing a nonconsenting state in its own courts to force compliance with the Fair Labor Standards Act of 1938.

The Court has held, however, that Congress may use Section 5 of the Fourteenth Amendment to authorize state employees to sue their employers in court for violations of the equal protection guarantees found in that Amendment.[35] In such legislation Congress must ensure that there is "congruence and proportionality "between the violation of the Fourteenth Amendment and the means used to remedy those violations. In a case from 2000, *Kimel v. Florida Board of Regents,* the Supreme Court prohibited employees of the State of Florida from suing the state for alleged violations of the Age Discrimination in Employment Act of 1967 (ADEA) because, the Court reasoned, Congress had exceeded its authority under the Fourteenth Amendment when it authorized such lawsuits.[36] The Court argued that "the substantive requirements the ADEA imposes on state . . . governments are disproportionate to any unconstitutional conduct that conceivably could be targeted by the Act" since "age is not a suspect classification."[37] In a similar case in 2001, *Board of Trustees of the University of Alabama v. Garrett,* the Court blocked an attempt by two state employees in Alabama to seek money damages for alleged violations of the 1990 Americans with Disabilities Act (ADA) by the state. When enacting the ADA, Congress relied on authority found in the Fourteenth Amendment, but the Court ruled that remedies called for under the ADA failed to meet the congruence and proportionality requirement since Congress had found no pattern of state-sponsored irrational employment discrimination against disabled persons prior to passage of the legislation.[38]

While the full ramifications of these decisions are not yet clear, they raise questions about the effectiveness of federal statutory law as a mechanism to combat discriminatory behavior by state governments. Perhaps state law itself will become the primary check against some forms of discriminatory behavior by state and local government institutions. If, under these circumstances, federal law provides less of an incentive for state governments to promote diversity, then an important impetus for affirmative action could be weakened.

The Growing Controversy in the 1990s

As previously discussed, the development of goals and timetables as an affirmative action strategy represented a significant change in our approach to the problem of discrimination. Because goals are formulated on the basis of race, ethnicity, or sex, and their development implies that preferences may be extended to members of minority groups or women when such individuals possess necessary qualifications, selection policies are not completely neutral when this approach to affirmative action is applied. In other words, goals and timetables require that race, ethnicity, or sex be taken into account in employment, college admissions, or government contracting decisions. As explained in chapter 1, and as also noted earlier in this chapter, this is the aspect of affirmative action that has proved to be most controversial, and the debate has persisted to one degree or another since the early 1970s. In that time, the affirmative action issue has permeated numerous political campaigns. The two major political parties have gradually split on the question, with Republicans now generally opposed to such programs and Democrats supportive of them, although Republicans during the Nixon years had embraced this approach.

All efforts to combat historical patterns of discrimination, including current affirmative action practices, are designed to give opportunity to those who have suffered or continue to suffer disadvantages and the denial of opportunity because of race or sex. Again, as was noted previously, if we are to move away from a situation in which discrimination works to exclude minorities and women to the condition where discrimination is no longer a barrier to the advancement of those groups, individuals who benefited under earlier circumstances (primarily nonminority males) may find that they face increased competition, which is why this issue is so contentious. Some of those individuals might be expected to be less than supportive of policies intended to bring about this change. Although most people will not oppose such programs as complaint processing and minority outreach, which are premised on notions of equality of opportunity, they might challenge programs involving preferences for women and minorities because those approaches transcend the principle of nondiscrimination.

Proposition 209

The emergence of a Republican majority in Congress in 1994, as well as conservative gains in state legislatures across the nation, helped to push the issue of affirmative action to a prominent position on the public agenda in the mid-1990s. In 1995, the Republican leadership in Congress advocated efforts to eliminate the use of affirmative action.[39] In response, the Clinton administration conducted a complete review of federal affirmative action programs and concluded that such approaches should be continued.[40] As we have also seen, considerable debate over the issue occurred place at the state level with the state of California figuring prominently in the struggle. A Republican governor, Pete Wilson, vigorously campaigned against affirmative action before election to a second term in 1994, and in 1995 the Regents of the University System of California voted to prohibit the consideration of race or gender as a factor in decisions regarding admissions to state universities. More significant, however, was the passage of Proposition 209 by California voters in November 1996. Proposition 209 was the ballot initiative that amended the state constitution to prohibit the use of preferences based on race, ethnicity, or gender associated with affirmative action. The substantive section of the proposal declared:

> Neither the State of California nor any of its political subdivisions or agents shall use race, sex, color, ethnicity, or national origin as a criterion for either discrimination against, or granting preferential treatment to, any individual or group in the operation of the State's public employment, public education, or public contracting.

The initiative was sponsored by various conservative political groups, but its primary architects were two white male academics who argued that their central purpose was to "restore true color-blind fairness in the United States."[41] Such a declaration obviously begs the question of whether "color-blind fairness" has ever really existed and could therefore be "restored." Nevertheless, the proposition was well received by a large audience and a prominent African American businessman, Ward Connerly, became an articulate and outspoken proponent of the initiative, arguing that strict equality of opportunity should prevail. Connerly was appointed chairman of the California Campaign for Proposition 209, and the campaign that he led attracted enormous attention from across the country. Ultimately, the proposal gathered the support of 54 percent of the California voters.

Shortly after Proposition 209 passed, the focus of the struggle over the initiative shifted to the legal arena. A challenge was filed in federal court alleging the initiative violated the equal protection component of the Fourteenth Amendment to the U.S. Constitution. The argument advanced by opponents of the measure was that because the proposition prohibited the state of California from engaging in affirmative action that included minority or female preferences, policy alternatives designed to benefit those groups were limited. In effect, barriers were erected against government aid to women and minorities, and thus members of those groups were denied equal protection of the laws. The District Court barred implementation of the proposition and ultimately ruled that it was unconstitutional, but a unanimous panel from the Ninth Circuit Court of Appeals ruled later that the District Court judge had erred and that Proposition 209 actually advanced the concept of equal protection by prohibiting preferential treatment. The prohibition on affirmative action goals and preferences in California was allowed to stand.

The success of California's Proposition 209 indicates that citizen initiatives can be effective tools against affirmative action. Soon after passage of Proposition 209, similar initiatives were introduced in several other states including Colorado, Florida, Massachusetts, Oregon, and Washington (see table 3.1). In most instances, however, these initiatives failed to gather substantial support. For example, a Republican political activist named Scott Marian drafted and introduced a Colorado Initiative on Civil Rights in 1995 but could not obtain the necessary signatures (50,000) within six months, and as a result, the measure was never placed on the Colorado ballot.[42] Also in 1995, fourteen individuals signed and submitted an initiative called "An Act to End Quotas and Promote True Equal Opportunity" in the Commonwealth of Massachusetts, but the endeavor never progressed beyond that stage. Oregonians for Equal Rights filed papers with, and received approval from, the secretary of state to circulate a petition for a proposed ballot initiative repealing provisions of state law requiring, encouraging, or

Table 3.1

State	Initiative
California	Proposition 209 provided that the state shall not discriminate against, or grant preferential treatment to, any individual or group on the basis of race, sex, color, ethnicity, or national origin in the operation of public employment, public education, or public contracting. Proposition 209 was passed by California Voters in November 1996.
Colorado	Proposed ballot initiative titled, "Repeal of Affirmative Action," filed in November 1995: Neither the State of Colorado nor any of its political subdivisions or agents shall consider the race, color, ethnicity, national origin, gender, or religion of any person as a factor in any decision pertaining to public employment, public education, or public contracting.
Florida	Proposed 1998 ballot initiative filed March 29, 1995, by The Campaign for Florida's Future. It proposed an amendment that would prohibit any affirmative action program by either the State of Florida or any political subdivision of the state in the areas of public employment, public education, and public contracting. It would also bar the state and its subdivision from any action that discriminates either in favor of or against any persons on the basis of race, sex, color, ethnicity, or national origin in those areas.
Massachusetts	Proposed ballot initiative titled, "An Act to End Quotas and Promote True Equal Opportunity," filed in 1995. It proposed an amendment that states: Neither the Commonwealth of Massachusetts nor any of its political subdivisions or agents shall use race, sex, color, ethnicity, or national origin as a criterion for either discriminating against, or granting preferential treatment to, any individual or group in the operation of the state's system of public employment, public education, or public contracting.
Oregon	Proposed 1996 ballot initiative filed June 2, 1995. It would have repealed provisions of the state law requiring, encouraging or resulting in reverse discrimination based on affirmative action, goals and timetables, or quotas and set-asides. The initiative prohibited the state and its political subdivisions from utilizing or compelling private citizens to utilize discrimination or preferences in education, employment, contracting or

Table 3.1, continued   provision of public services. The text was approved to circulate, but the requisite number of signatures was never received.

Washington   Ballot Initiative 200 was filed on March 26, 1997. The Washington State Civil Rights Initiative prohibits state and local government entities from discriminating against, or granting preferential treatment to, any individual or group based on race, sex, color, ethnicity, or national origin in public employment, public education, and public contracting. The initiative was passed by Washington voters in November 1998.

Ballot Initiative 172, titled the Anti-discrimination and Anti-preferential Treatment Act of 1996, would have prohibited the state of Washington or any of its political subdivisions or agents from using race, sex, color, ethnicity, national origin, or status as a sexual minority as a criterion for granting preferential treatment to any individual or group.

Source: Adapted from J. Edward Kellough, Sally Coleman Selden, and Jerome S. Legge, Jr., "Affirmative Action under Fire: The Current Controversy and the Potential for State Policy Retrenchment," *Review of Public Personnel Administration,* vol. xvii, no. 4 (fall 1997), Table 4, pp. 67–68.

---

resulting in reverse discrimination based on affirmative action, goals and timetables, or quotas and set-asides. However, questions circulated regarding the authenticity of some signatures, and the grassroots organization never formally submitted the collected signatures to the secretary of state for verification.

The Washington Ballot Initiative

The major exception to this pattern was the Washington Ballot Initiative (I-200), filed in March 1997, which gained substantial support and significant attention in the media. It was modeled directly after California's Proposition 209 and appeared on the state ballot in November 1998. The initiative passed with the support of 58 percent of the voters, making Washington the second state to prohibit racial, ethnic, or gender preferences in state employment, contracting, or higher education.

A leading proponent of this initiative was Republican state representative Scott Smith, a former insurance agent, whose fight against affirmative action started years earlier when he introduced legislation in the state legislature to repeal the use of preferences. Smith reportedly supported recruitment efforts to increase minority and female access to programs but opposed the use of quotas, preferences, and goals. Apparently, Smith had enough votes in the House and Senate in 1997 to pass a bill banning the use of preferences in public education, employment, and contracting. However, concern among some anti-affirmative action strategists that Washington's Democratic Governor Gary Locke (the first Chinese-American governor of a state) would veto a bill restricting affirmative action led Senate Majority Leader Dan McDonald to ask Smith to pursue the bill as an initiative rather than as legislation.[43] Not only did the initiative process allow voters to voice their preferences, but the process also bypassed the governor.

To devote his full attention to the initiative campaign and to coordinate the collection of the 180,000 signatures required to bring the measure to the state legislature and ultimately to the 1998 ballot, Representative Smith sold his insurance company and committed his full attention to the endeavor. The signature campaign also benefited significantly from support by Ward Connerly, the vocal critic of affirmative action and former chairman of the Proposition 209 campaign in California. Connerly's organization, the American Civil Rights Institute, provided logistic and financial support to assist organizers in gathering the necessary signatures. More than twenty groups were contracted to collect 10,000 signatures each. Most groups were Republican legislative district clubs, but others included conservative associations such as the Evergreen Republican Women's Club, the Chelan-Douglas Women's Club, the Eastside Young Republicans, Spokane County Young Republicans, the South Kitsap Women's Club, the Coalition for Public Trust, the Reform Party, and the Tax Reform Party. Ultimately, the extensive work of these groups was critical to the success of the measure.[44]

Anti-affirmative action efforts also spread to legislative assemblies across the nation during these years. In the mid- to late 1990s, a number of Republican members of Congress urged passage of a "civil rights bill" that would end federal government affirmative action efforts. A study from that period examining the extent of the anti-affirmative action movement also found that as many as fifteen states had the issue placed on their legislative agendas in 1997, at a time when anti-affirmative action rhetoric was reaching a high point.[45] To provide some insight into the nature and extent of these proposals, table 3.2, which is adapted from that study, details the nature of these proposals to limit, ban, or weaken the use of preferential affirmative action policies.

Table 3.2

State	Legislative Proposals
Alabama	S. 477: Proposed a constitutional amendment, subject to voter approval, providing that the state could not discriminate against, or grant preferential treatment to, any individual or group on the basis of race, sex, color, ethnicity, or national origin in the operation of public employment, public education, or public contracting.
Arizona	H.C.R. 2008: Proposed a constitutional amendment, subject to voter approval, prohibiting discrimination against and preferential treatment to any individual or group on the basis of race, sex, color, ethnicity, or national origin in public employment, public education, or public contracting.
Arizona	H.C.R. 2223: The bill would have revised Title 41, Chapter 9, by adding an article prohibiting discrimination against, or preferential treatment to, an individual or group on the basis or race, sex, color, ethnicity, or national origin in the operation of public employment, public education, or public contracting.
Colorado	H.B. 97-1299: The Equal Opportunity Act of 1997 would have required that all state agencies conduct state business without regard to the race or gender of any person or entity. The term minority subcontractor was changed to emerging small business for purposes of considering the involvement of such entities in the criteria used to rank persons for state professional services contracts. The act also would have repealed state personnel board rules on affirmative action, except for grievance and appeal procedures based on allegations of discrimination.
Colorado	H.B. 97-1336: The act included a provision that would allow the voters of Colorado to approve or reject the prohibition of unlawful affirmative action by constitutional amendment at the next biennial regular general election.
Georgia	SB 243: The act would have amended Chapter 2 of Title 1 of the Official Code of Georgia Annotated to prohibit the State of Georgia, its agents, or any of its political subdivisions from using race, sex, color, creed, gender, or national origin as a criterion for either discriminating against or granting preferential treatment to any individual or group.

Text continues on p. 61.

Massachusetts	H.B. 2981: The act would have prohibited discrimination on the basis of race, color, national origin or primary language, sex, sexual orientation, religion, creed, age, or physical or mental handicap in programs funded by the Commonwealth of Massachusetts.
Michigan	H.B. 4459: The act would have prohibited the state from establishing a prebid qualification that bidders on state contracts have an affirmative action plan.
Mississippi	S.B. 2161: The act provided that the ability to seek employment is a constitutional right that shall not be unreasonably restricted.
Missouri	S.J.R. 3: Proposed to allow electors to vote on a constitutional amendment in November 1998 that stated: Neither the state nor any of its political subdivisions or agents shall discriminate against, or grant preferential treatment to, any individual or group on the basis of race, sex, color, ethnicity, or national origin as a criterion in the operation of public employment, public education, or public contracting.
Montana	H.B. 299: Proposed a constitutional amendment, subject to voter approval, prohibiting the state or any local government entity or subdivision of the state from granting preferential treatment to an individual or group on the basis of race, color, ethnicity, national origin, or sex in public employment, public education, or public contracting.
Montana	H.B. 303: The bill would have prohibited preferential treatment in employment, education, and contracting by state government, local government, public schools, and public post secondary educational institutions based on race, color, ethnicity, national origin, or sex.
New Jersey	A.B. 2533: The act would have prohibited public and certain private affirmative action programs based upon race, ethnicity, sex, color, or national origin. It read in part:

> the Legislature finds and declares that all officially sanctioned discrimination based upon characteristics such as race, religion, ethnicity, and national origin is contrary to the basic tenets of American society. Individual merit, not membership in a favored or disfavored group, is the only reasonable basis for differentiation between people. It is fundamentally unjust

for any individual to suffer an officially mandated burden, or to obtain an unjustified and unmerited benefit, solely on the basis of one's membership in an ethnic or racial class. Quotas, goals, set-asides, preferences, or other methods for taking irrational and irrelevant considerations like race or ethnicity into account are contrary to basic notions of fairness, justice, and fair play. Neither any public entity of the State of New Jersey nor any entity receiving public funds shall use race, ethnicity, sex, color, or national origin as a basis for awarding any preferences to an applicant for employment, for promotion, for admission to school, or any other benefit. Any private entity which is authorized or directed, by law enacted prior to the effective date of this act, to grant any preference on the basis of race, ethnicity, sex, color, or national origin shall cease to grant such preference as of that effective date.

New Jersey	A.B. 2748: Would have replaced preferences based upon race, ethnicity, national origin, or gender in affirmative action programs with preference for persons who are economically disadvantaged.
New York	A.B. 4534: Proposed a constitutional amendment, subject to voter approval, prohibiting discrimination or preferential treatment on account of race, sex, color, ethnicity, or national origin.
New York	S. 1722: Proposed a constitutional amendment, subject to voter approval, prohibiting discrimination or preferential treatment on account of race, sex, color, ethnicity, or national origin.
North Carolina	H.B. 981: Proposed a constitutional amendment, to be submitted to the electors, that would have prohibited the State from discriminating against, or granting preferential treatment to, any individual or group on the basis of race, gender, color, ethnicity, or national origin in the operation of public employment, public education, or public contracting.
Oklahoma	H.J.R 1010: Directed the Secretary of State to refer to the people for their approval or rejection a constitutional amendment providing for the elimination of affirmative action.
South Carolina	H. 3132: Proposed a constitutional amendment, subject to the approval of the electors, that would have prohibited the State of South Carolina or any of its political subdivisions from using race, sex, color, ethnicity, or national origin as a criteri-

Table 3.2, continued

	on for either discriminating against, or granting preferential treatment to, any individual or group in the operation of the State's system of public employment, public education, or public contracting.
South Carolina	S.B. 235: A bill to amend Title 1, Chapter 1, Code of Laws of South Carolina that adds Article 21, enacting the South Carolina Civil Rights Act. The act would have prohibited the State of South Carolina or any of its political subdivisions from using race, sex, color, ethnicity, or national origin as a criterion for either discriminating against, or granting preferential treatment to, any individual or group in the operation of the State's system of public employment, public education, or public contracting.

Source: Adapted from J. Edward Kellough, Sally Coleman Selden, and Jerome S. Legge, Jr., "Affirmative Action under Fire: The Current Controversy and the Potential for State Policy Retrenchment," *Review of Public Personnel Administration*, vol. xvii, no. 4 (fall 1997), Table 2, pp. 59–62.

As illustrated in table 3.2, nine states, Alabama, Arizona, Colorado, Missouri, Montana, New York, North Carolina, Oklahoma, and South Carolina proposed constitutional amendments to be approved by the state's electorate that would prohibit discrimination against or preferential treatment for an individual or group on the basis of race, sex, color, ethnicity, or national origin. In Colorado, Republican Representative Mark Paschall introduced HB 1336 as an initiative to be submitted directly to the Colorado voters bypassing Democratic Governor Roy Romer, who had promised to veto any direct legislative termination of affirmative action. The language used in Colorado HB 1336 and most of the other efforts mirrored the language of California's Proposition 209. Similar proposals were introduced in Georgia's House and Senate to amend the Official Code of Georgia; however, Georgia also included creed as a criterion.

Proposals in other states also had negative implications for affirmative action. In some instances, they were no doubt spurred in part by litigation, such as the *Hopwood* case overturning preferential policies in the Fifth Circuit. In Mississippi, an act was introduced, for example, declaring that an individual's ability to seek employment was a constitutional right that should not be unreasonably restricted by the state. In Massachusetts, House

Bill 2981 would have banned discrimination on the basis of race, color, national origin or primary language, sex, sexual orientation, religion, creed, age, or physical or mental handicaps in all programs funded by the Commonwealth. The bill did not specifically address or prohibit "preferential treatment" or affirmative action, but it was clear that the legislation was intended as an anti-affirmative action measure.

Ultimately, none of the bills listed in table 3.2 was passed into law, but state legislative activity on this issue in 1997 was indicative of opposition directed toward preferential affirmative action policies in the late 1990s. An examination of a number of state demographic and political variables suggests that a possible explanation for the introduction of this legislation in some states but not in others is the size of the state's minority population. Analysis reveals that states with larger minority populations were significantly more likely than states with smaller minority populations to have considered the repeal of affirmative action.[46] Of course, in states with small minority populations, affirmative action is less likely to be an issue. In addition, legislators may introduce bills, even those that they do not expect will pass, for a variety of idiosyncratic reasons. Nevertheless, some nonminority legislators from states with larger minority populations may find political advantage with their nonminority constituents by opposing affirmative action.

Many state governors also officially addressed the question of affirmative action during the 1990s. Table 3.3 presents information concerning gubernatorial executive orders issued in the 1990s on the matter. Interestingly, of the thirteen orders issued, only those by California Governor Pete Wilson, Louisiana Governor Mike Foster, and Florida Governor Jeb Bush limited state affirmative action programs. As suggested earlier, Governor Wilson's position on affirmative action may have been an important factor in the broader campaign to overturn the use of preferences in California. In Louisiana, Governor Foster provided that race and sex could be considered in decisions to allocate public educational, contractual, employment, economic, and other opportunities, but they could not serve as determining factors. Moreover, he ordered that Louisiana eliminate any statutes or regulations that authorize the use of quotas or guaranteed outcomes based on race and/or sex. Governor Foster argued that Martin Luther King, Jr. would have been an opponent of affirmative action. In a

Table 3.3

GUBERNATORIAL EXECUTIVE ORDERS ADDRESSING

AFFIRMATIVE ACTION IN THE 1990S.

State	Executive Order
Alaska	E.O. 78 transferred the Office of Equal Employment from the Office of the Governor to the Department of Administration and affirmed Governor Tony Knowles' commitment to affirmative action programs.
California	In May 1995, Governor Pete Wilson issued an executive order that repealed affirmative action requirements not required by state law or federal mandate.
Colorado	In 1987, Governor Roy Romer issued an executive order declaring Colorado's commitment to equal employment opportunity and affirmative action. On August 22, 1995, Governor Romer reiterated his commitment to this executive order, and outlined a new diversity plan for state employment.
Delaware	On March 10, 1995, Governor Thomas R. Carper issued Executive Order 28 proclaiming that "the State of Delaware's commitment to equal employment opportunity is hereby affirmed and all heads of Executive Branch Agencies are directed to pursue diligently the recruitment of qualified women and minorities and to be vigilant in complying with the laws prohibiting discrimination in employment." The Governor also created the Governor's Council on Equal Employment Opportunity to monitor and evaluate agencies' implementation of and compliance with Executive Order 28. The Order requires that the head of each Executive Branch Agency maintain an Affirmative Action Plan that includes a specific statement of goals and objectives designed to assure employment opportunities in hiring and promotion and to eliminate any unlawful discrimination in Agency employment as well as a specific statement of action steps designed to remedy any problem of underrepresentation of minorities and women that may exist in the Agency.
Florida	Governor Jeb Bush issued an executive order on November 9, 1999, eliminating affirmative action preferences in state contracts and employment and encouraging the state Board of Regents to prohibit affirmative action in admission policies of state universities.

Text continues on p. 66.

Georgia   On April 16, 1992, Governor Zell Miller signed an executive
                 order that required all state agencies, authorities, commissions
                 and institutions to increase access and participation of minor-
                 ity businesses in state contracting.

Louisiana   In Executive Order MJF 96-2, Governor Mike Foster stated:
                 "It is the policy of the State of Louisiana to advance inclusion,
                 impartiality, mutual understanding, and respect for diversity
                 among all people, without regard to race or gender; it is the
                 policy of the State of Louisiana, in accordance with rulings by
                 the United States Supreme Court, that race and gender may
                 be considered in decisions to allocate educational, contractual,
                 employment, economic, and other opportunities in this state,
                 but that these factors shall not be the deciding or predominant
                 factors in such decisions unless required or mandated by fed-
                 eral statutes, regulations, or court orders; and it is the policy of
                 the State of Louisiana to eliminate any statutes or regulations
                 authorizing quotas or guaranteeing outcomes based only on
                 race or gender except as required by federal statutes, regula-
                 tion or court orders."

Massachusetts   In E.O. 96-390, Governor William Weld declared that "It is the
                 policy of the Commonwealth to promote equality in the mar-
                 ketplace and, to that end, to encourage full participation of
                 minority and women owned businesses in all areas of state con-
                 tracting, including contracts for construction, design, goods,
                 and services. The Commonwealth has a compelling interest in
                 using racial and gender based classifications for the purposes
                 of remedying past discrimination and promoting other, non-
                 remedial objectives, such as the delivery of effective human
                 services in the areas of public health, safety, and welfare."

Michigan   In Executive Order 1996-13, Governor John Engler stated: "It
                 is the continuing policy of this administration to ensure equal
                 opportunity in the recruitment, selection, promotion and re-
                 tention of all state classified employees; it is the desire of the
                 State of Michigan and this Governor to increase active mea-
                 sures that promote equal employment opportunity in state
                 government to foster a diverse work force."

Missouri   Governor Mel Carnahan issued E.O. 94-03 to provide that all
                 present and prospective state employees are afforded equal op-
                 portunity at all levels and phases of employment to include

but not limited to hiring, recruiting, training, benefits, promotions, transfers, layoffs, demotions, terminations, rate of compensation, and recalls from layoffs. Each department is required to file a revised Affirmative Action Plan with the State EEO officer. Each plan is to include: a departmental policy statement on EEO and AA; a statistical utilization and availability analysis that will contain a work force analysis, job group analysis, and availability analysis; an identification of underutilization; goals and timetables for the present and future; an identification of problem areas and corrective actions to be taken; documentation of internal audit and reporting systems; internal grievance procedures; a copy of recruiting practices; and identification and implementation of diversity training.

Oregon

In Executive Order 96-38, Governor John Kitzhaber expressed his commitment to affirmative action. He directed all state agency directors and administrators to submit reports on the status and results of their affirmative action policies and programs to his office. Moreover, Governor Kitzhaber incorporated affirmative action efforts and results into the performance evaluation of managers. He mandated that the departments of Transportation and Corrections shall work with his office to increase minority and female representation in the construction activities of Oregon.

Pennsylvania

In Executive Order 1996-9, Governor Thomas Ridge stated that no agency under the jurisdiction of the Governor shall discriminate against any employee or applicant for employment because of race, color, religious creed, ancestry, union membership, age, sex, sexual orientation, national origin, AIDS or HIV status, or disability. Positive steps shall be taken by each agency under the jurisdiction of the Governor to ensure fair and equal employment at every level of government for African Americans, Hispanics, Asians, American Indians, Alaskans, Pacific Islanders, persons with a disability, persons of 40 years of age or older, and women. The Governor also designated the Secretary of Administration to supervise the development, implementation, and enforcement of the Commonwealth's equal employment opportunity programs through the Bureau of Equal Employment Opportunity.

Virginia

In Executive Order 1994-2, Governor George Allen prohibited discrimination on the basis of race, sex, color, national origin,

Table 3.3, continued

religion, age, or political affiliation, or against otherwise qualified persons with disabilities. Governor Allen directed all ap-
pointing authorities and other management principals to take
affirmative measures, as determined by the Director, Department of Personnel and Training, to emphasize the recruitment of qualified minorities, women, disabled persons, and
older Virginians to serve at all levels of state government. This
directive does not permit or require the lowering of bona fide
job requirements, performance standards, or qualifications to
give preference to any state employee or applicant for state
employment.

Source: Adapted from J. Edward Kellough, Sally Coleman Selden, and Jerome S. Legge, Jr., "Affirmative
Action under Fire: The Current Controversy and the Potential for State Policy Retrenchment," *Review
of Public Personnel Administration*, vol. xvii, no. 4 (fall 1997), Table 3, pp. 63–65.

---

newspaper interview, Foster stated: "I can't find anywhere in his writings
that he wanted reverse discrimination. He just wanted an end to all discrimination based on color."[47] Foster made opposition to affirmative action "quotas" a centerpiece in his campaign for the governorship.

The One Florida Initiative

The executive order issued by Governor Bush of Florida became a centerpiece of what was known as the "One Florida Initiative." The order eliminated affirmative action preferences in state contracts and employment
and encouraged the Board of Regents of the State University System to implement a similar policy for admissions to state universities.[48] In announcing the initiative, Governor Bush argued that his plan would bring an end
to "racial preferences, racial set-asides, and race-based university admissions," but it would not end affirmative action "properly understood."[49]
Presumably, outreach efforts for minority employment and participation
in contracting would continue. The governor proposed that race-neutral
factors such as "income level, whether an applicant is a first generation college student, and geographical diversity" would continue to be considered
in the process of making decisions regarding admission to state colleges and
universities. Additionally, the governor proposed a program that would
guarantee college admission to the top 20 percent of seniors in every high
school in the state and a program that would increase need-based financial

assistance to students by 43 percent. In the governor's words, the One Florida Initiative "transcends traditional notions of affirmative action."[50]

Governor Bush's initiative might have been presented to deter an effort to place an anti-affirmative action amendment before Florida voters in the year 2000. That effort was being financed by Florida contractors and led by Ward Connerly, the chief proponent of the California initiative.[51] In mid-January of 2000, two members of the Florida State Legislature, Senator Kendrick Meek and Representative Anthony Hill, occupied the office of Lieutenant Governor Frank Brogan to protest the governor's order. After twenty-four hours of intense discussions, an agreement was reached with Governor Bush that the University System Board of Regents would delay consideration of the portion of the order addressing higher education until February 17, 2000. The delay would allow time for three legislative hearings and further public discussion of the possible effects of the proposed changes on minority enrollment in Florida's state colleges and universities. The governor issued a statement summarizing the agreement on January 19, 2000, but the agreement did not address or affect in any manner the sections of Executive Order 99-281 dealing with state contracting or state employment.[52]

Proponents of affirmative action might take some comfort in the fact that ten of the thirteen governors issuing executive orders addressing affirmative action during the 1990s were supportive of the policy. Efforts ranged from Georgia Governor Zell Miller's support for increasing access and participation of minority businesses in state contracting to full-blown support for affirmative action programs by governors in Missouri and Pennsylvania. Although the political culture of Virginia is relatively conservative and its governor was a Republican, legislation to dismantle affirmative action programs was not introduced during the 1995 or 1997 legislative sessions. This interesting development may reflect Republican legislators' deference to Governor George Allen, who endorsed equal opportunity and affirmative action measures at the beginning of his administration.

The Rise of Diversity Management

As affirmative action came increasingly under attack in the mid-1990s, new programs emphasizing "diversity" or "diversity management" began to emerge. To a considerable extent, the popularity of diversity programs was a reaction to, or a response to, the rise in opposition to affirmative action.[53] As we have seen, preferential affirmative action was an easy target for criticism. Diversity programs, on the other hand, were presumably less controversial. Diversity management was based on notions of inclusiveness and the need to recognize the value of all individuals. The rhetoric of diversity was that differences should be valued, and that organizations should be managed in a way that allows people from all backgrounds to succeed. Such language stood in sharp contrast to the preferential approaches to affirmative action. Beleaguered supporters of traditional equal employment opportunity and affirmative action could take refuge in the diversity management paradigm, and that is precisely what many of them did as the decade of the 1990s advanced.

A 1999 survey of federal government agencies provides some insight into this phenomenon.[54] As early as 1993, the U.S. Merit Systems Protection Board found little evidence that federal government organizations had developed diversity management programs.[55] By 1999, however, 88 percent of federal agencies and subagencies claimed to operate diversity management initiatives of some type.[56] Interestingly, however, of those who made that claim, 25 percent indicated that they had essentially changed the names of their equal employment opportunity and affirmative action programs to diversity management.[57] Others argued, however, that their diversity management programs were more broadly based and included activities not typically found in traditional affirmative action programs such as employee training designed to promote an understanding of and appreciation for diversity. These federal organizations often attempted to stress that diversity was not to be defined simply in terms of race, ethnicity, or gender, but that it encompassed all of the ways in which people are different. Even in these programs, however, traditional functions that were usually associated with affirmative action efforts, such as minority recruitment or the establishment of minority employment goals, were core aspects of the initiative.[58]

Of course, diversity management was not sold merely as a back-door way to pursue an affirmative action agenda. Diversity advocates usually argued strenuously that their efforts were distinct from, and indeed transcended, affirmative action, and in many cases, their claims were undoubtedly true.[59] In fact, R. Roosevelt Thomas, who is credited with first using the phrase "diversity management," was sharply critical of affirmative action in his early work. Achievements under affirmative action had been "stupendous," Thomas wrote in 1990, but he argued that increasingly its ideas were looking "shopworn."[60] "Sooner or later," wrote Thomas, "affirmative action will die a natural death."[61] Presumably, diversity management would replace controversial and divisive affirmative action programs.

Despite such assertions, a fundamental ambiguity exists as to what diversity management actually means. On the one hand, it may be quite different from affirmative action and may be seen as a successor to those programs. Thomas argued that the goal in the 1990s was to "manage diversity to get from [it] the same productivity we once got from a homogenous work force, and to do it without artificial programs, standards—or barriers."[62] This argument suggests that diversity management is about more effectively managing organizations that have already achieved diversity. Thomas also asserted that diversity encompassed more than racial, ethnic, or gender differences, and that it should be defined in terms of any mixture of attributes that distinguish people, including such characteristics as age, education, background, or personality. In this way, diversity is inclusive and is easily distinguished from affirmative action. On the other hand, however, much of what Thomas advocated looked very much like traditional affirmative action. For example, Thomas argued that organizations should be managed in such a way that diversity is created by utilizing recruitment and outreach efforts to increase the presence of minorities in organizations.[63]

This duality of purpose or orientation is reflected in the diversity literature, as well as in programmatic activities. In some cases, diversity management is defined as strategies by which diversity is more carefully managed within an organization so that all employees are able to achieve their full potential. Managers and employees are trained to appreciate diversity and, to put it simply, to work well with others. An emphasis is placed on cooperation, conflict resolution, and the creation of an internal environment that is open and hospitable to all. In other situations, diversity management appears to be interpreted to mean managing in such a way as to create or establish diversity in organizations where it is lacking. Such an approach would rely, for example, on recruitment or outreach programs designed to attract employees from diverse backgrounds. Of course, these alternative interpretations are not entirely distinct, since efforts to establish hospitable internal organizational environments may have the added effect of making the organizational environment more attractive to people from diverse backgrounds and, as a result, may help to further achieve diversity.

Within the field of management, ideas come and go. Concepts or approaches are conceived with good intentions, are endorsed by scholars, are advocated by consultants, rise in popularity, and then recede from view to be replaced by the next insight, innovation, or approach. Management by Objectives, Total Quality Management, Quality Circles, and "Theory Z" all stand as markers of this pattern of behavior. Whether diversity management will become yet another example of this phenomenon remains to be seen. If the controversy over affirmative action recedes, the need to sell those efforts with the diversity label will be reduced. But if the affirmative action controversy endures or increases, diversity programs may also come under attack to the extent that they are repackaged affirmative action programs. In either case, diversity management may fade from the position of prominence it currently enjoys in the world of human resources management.

Showing whether diversity management programs can be unambiguously effective will also be crucial. The literature on diversity programs contains surprisingly little empirical work on that question, however. Most of that literature consists of essays advocating for diversity management programs or discussions of the types of practices that should be part of those efforts. How the authors are able to identify those "best" practices absent systematic work on the impact of diversity management programs is certainly a subject open to question. One of the few studies that deals with the issue of whether diversity programs have made any measurable difference within organizations has come to a rather pessimistic set of conclusions.[64] In that research, federal diversity management programs noted earlier were examined. A set of indices was constructed to measure the level of development of agency diversity programs in a general sense and in several specific dimensions indicated by the presence of programmatic elements identified in the literature as important for diversity management success. Significant variation among federal agencies was found. Scores on the general index, for example, which were based on a summary of standardized scores for specific programmatic components, varied widely—with the U.S. Coast Guard registering high on all indicators of program development and other agencies (such as the Internal Revenue Service, the Drug Enforcement Administration, and the Economic Development Administration) within the Commerce Department obtaining extremely low scores. Once this variation was observed, the question was whether agencies with more highly developed programs were producing better results than those with weaker programs. Because diversity management efforts are intended, at least in part, to create internal organizational environments supportive of people from diverse backgrounds that will enable all employees to succeed to their fullest extent, the research sought to measure the effectiveness of diversity management by examining the impact of personnel policies in federal agencies on minorities and women. Specifically, the work looked at the promotions of minorities and women, African American dismissal rates, and African American quit rates. The assumption was that if diversity programs had achieved more equitable work environments, then each of these measures would be proportional to the presence in the organization work force of the groups specified. For example, the minority share of promotions was expected to be approximately equal to the minority share of the work force in the pay grades under examination when an equitable environment was obtained. African American quits and dismissals were examined similarly. In general, the findings showed that agencies with more highly developed diversity management programs did not produce more equitable outcomes on the measures specified than agencies with less developed programs, when the effects of traditional affirmative action programs predating diversity management efforts were controlled statistically.[65]

Conclusion

Considerable opposition to affirmative action has emerged in the United States in the past decade. The policy has been under attack in many state capitols, and opponents have achieved several notable victories. Numerous politicians have called for the repeal of affirmative action. In a few states, citizens have come together in opposition to affirmative action programs. Supporters of affirmative action in many states have been placed in a defensive position.

One encouraging development, from the perspective of affirmative action's proponents, however, was the failure of a local, anti–affirmative action ballot initiative in Houston, Texas, in November of 1997. The proposal would have banned any preferential affirmative action by the city, but it was firmly rejected. Additionally, the state of Texas has also figured prominently in the struggle over affirmative action in another way. The state's attorney general, Dan Morales, issued a legal opinion in February 1996 banning the use of affirmative action in college and university admissions, recruiting, and scholarships. The action was taken in response to the U.S. Fifth Circuit Court of Appeals decision in the case *Hopwood v. State of Texas* (1996) in which the Court determined that race could not be used as a factor in university admissions. Attorney General Morales ruled that Texas public universities must employ only race-neutral criteria in administering their internal policies, including admissions, financial aid, scholarships, fellowships, recruitment, and retention.[66] In what may have been an effort to ease the impact of this restriction on affirmative action programs in university admissions, legislation was enacted that required the thirty-five public universities in Texas to admit all students in the top 10 percent of high school graduating classes from accredited high schools.[67] This program appears to have been a model for part of the educational reform associated with the initiative by Jeb Bush, governor of Florida and brother of President George W. Bush, who at that time was governor of Texas.

The policies that have been the target of most anti–affirmative action efforts are those permitting or requiring the use of numerical goals or preferences designed to benefit minorities and women. This focus can be seen in the language of proposals calling for the elimination of preferences or the prohibition of the consideration of race, ethnicity, or gender to either discriminate against or in favor of any individual. Advocates of these types of reforms are seeking to shift policies to what they perceive as a foundation built on a strict view of nondiscrimination and equality of opportunity. Advocates for affirmative action are effectively forced to argue in favor of policies that, in the view of many observers, violate notions of nondiscrimination. Compared to the relatively simple case made out by affirmative action's opponents, this can be a difficult argument to present.

What will be left of affirmative action if goals and preferential policies are eliminated? In that situation, future programs would likely resemble affirmative action typical of the early 1960s based largely on minority outreach or recruitment efforts. Employers, for example, could still work to attract minorities or women into their pool of applicants, but actual selection decisions would be required to be free from the consideration of race or sex. Whether such policies would be effective in overcoming discrimination against women and minority group members is open to debate. One factor that may work to the advantage of minorities, however, is the ever-increasing racial and ethnic diversity in the United States. As minorities become a larger segment of the population nationally, many organizations may find increased advantages in drawing on the talents and abilities of all people regardless of race or ethnic background. The ways in which this diversity will ultimately operate, and the effectiveness of future efforts to combat discrimination, are yet to be revealed. Of course, proponents of affirmative action were handed a major victory in the summer of 2003 when the U.S. Supreme Court upheld the affirmative action program associated with admissions policies at the University of Michigan School of Law.[68] The next chapter will summarize arguments for and against affirmative action. Following that discussion, the important role of the courts will be considered.

four

Assessing the Argument
A Review of the Case For and Against Affirmative Action

As has been stressed a number of times in this work, affirmative action encompasses a variety of efforts to benefit members of groups, primarily racial and ethnic minorities and women, who have been historically disadvantaged because of discrimination. Affirmative action includes outreach and recruitment efforts, as well as the establishment of goals for the selection of individuals from underrepresented groups and the preferences that are implicit in those goals. While the purpose has been to counter historical patterns of discrimination and injustice, affirmative action has been immersed in controversy since its inception. To a considerable extent, the debate centers on a conflict between two competing values that are fundamental to American political culture: equality and liberty. All parties in the struggle over affirmative action embrace both values to some degree, but proponents of the policy tend to emphasize equality, or more specifically, equality of opportunity for groups historically disadvantaged, while opponents prefer liberty in the sense that employers and others should be free to select whomever they believe is best suited for available positions without special consideration for or against women or any group defined in terms of race or ethnicity. This chapter will not resolve that debate. The purpose here is to review the underlying rationale for affirmative action, to consider the arguments offered by opponents of the policy, and to assess the arguments on both sides of the issue.

The Fundamental Arguments for Affirmative Action

Several arguments are offered in defense of affirmative action. They are based on the belief that justice demands an end to the discrimination that has disadvantaged minorities and women, that affirmative action is just compensation for past and current discrimination, and that integration and diversity promoted through affirmative action are instrumental to achieving valuable outcomes for organizations and society at large. All arguments presume, of course, that affirmative action will be effective in its objective of working to the benefit of women and minorities.

Affirmative Action as Justice:
Redistributive and Compensatory Arguments

Because affirmative action evolved as a part of the struggle to combat discrimination against racial and ethnic minorities and women, its justification rests, at least initially, on the legitimacy of that struggle. Most observers would agree that efforts to overcome historical patterns of racial injustice are necessary. In other words, most people in this country would accept the proposition that justice demands that work to overcome discrimination against minorities and women and its various consequences is needed. Clearly, this has not always been the case, and even now some people of a more libertarian bent see no role at all for government in that effort. For example, Richard Epstein has argued that laws prohibiting discrimination are undesirable because they impose inefficiencies on organizations, and they are essentially unnecessary in a free market. Not only would Epstein end affirmative action, he would also repeal nondiscrimination laws such as the Civil Rights Act of 1964 and other similar statutes. In Epstein's view, discrimination against women and minorities wastes valuable resources, and a free market will eventually eliminate discrimination.[1] While this argument is interesting, it is ultimately unpersuasive. As Cass Sunstein has noted, free markets will not prevent discrimination when discriminatory behavior is consistent with the preferences of an organization's employees or clients, or when it is seen as an acceptable alternative to bearing the costs of obtaining individualized information about job applicants.[2] In general, the discussion of racial and sexual justice and the struggle for equality have developed to the point that most people understand the tragic results of historic patterns of discriminatory behavior and are unwilling to leave the resolution of discriminatory practices to the nuances of the labor market. Proponents of affirmative action argue that if we are to become a society in which the problem of discrimination is overcome, and minorities and women have the full range of opportunities that are enjoyed by nonminority men, then we must effectively counter discrimination directed against those groups.[3] A redistribution of opportunity is necessary, according to this way of thinking, so that those who have been excluded in the past or those who are currently excluded will be fully included. Indeed, not until the government became active in the struggle to overcome discrimination was significant progress made. Affirmative action is an outgrowth of that effort.

Because unjust discrimination has restricted opportunities for minorities and women, many people have also argued that justice demands some form of compensation for losses suffered, not simply the cessation of discrimination and an equitable distribution of current opportunity. This is an argument for compensatory justice, which requires that amends be made for past and current inequities. Howard McGary, Jr., for example, has argued that African Americans are entitled to preferential treatment in employment and admission to institutions of higher education as reparation for centuries of injustice they have suffered.[4] Relatedly, Samuel Krislov draws on the analogy of a race in which two runners are competing, but one is forced to physically bear a heavy burden. After the race has progressed, and the unencumbered runner is far ahead, you cannot, according to Krislov, look to the one carrying the burden and say, "I see the injustice you are suffering, you may now drop the burden by the side of the course," and believe that you have made the race equal. Some restitution must be made for the prior injustice.[5] In his famous Commencement address at Howard University in June 1965, President Johnson used a similar analogy to defend affirmative action: "You do not take a person who, for years, has been hobbled by chains and liberate him, bring him to the starting line of a race, and then say, 'you are free to compete with all the others,' and still justly believe you have been completely fair."[6] In the years since Johnson's remarks, compensatory justice has become a core argument in defense of affirmative action.[7]

Utilitarian Arguments: The Value of Diversity

An additional set of arguments for efforts to combat discrimination that has operated to disadvantage African Americans, Hispanics, and others rests not so much on notions of redistributive or compensatory justice, but on the belief that integration and diversity within organizations brings broadly desirable outcomes.[8] In work settings, for example, organizations that hire a diversity of employees will, as a consequence, include within their ranks individuals with diverse perspectives and ways of dealing with organizational tasks. This is so because racial, ethnic, and gender identities carry with them distinctive socialization experiences that often result in diverse values and perspectives. While all employees, regardless of background, must obviously be socialized to accept their organization's fundamental mission, the presence of a diversity of views as to the best tactical and strategic approaches to achieve that mission may help to ensure that effective options are not overlooked and that a wider range of possibilities is considered than would be the case if the organization were staffed homogeneously.[9] In this sense, diversity is clearly valuable. It builds strength within the organization, and it may lead to greater productivity or improved performance, especially when an organization or group is confronted with a series of difficult or complicated tasks.

A number of empirical studies have confirmed the positive association between diversity and work-group performance, although the relationship is typically moderated by such factors as the length of time a diverse group has worked together and the complexity of work assignments. For example, research has shown that when groups are newly formed, diversity creates conditions that can inhibit group interaction processes and group effectiveness.[10] However, as diverse or heterogeneous groups continue to work together across time, they typically are able to adjust to their differences, develop effective interaction and communication processes, and succeed at a level beyond that of homogeneous groups in efforts to deal with complex situations. In general then, racial, ethnic, and sex diversity creates a diversity of information and perspectives that can ultimately be beneficial. A diverse group's success, however, will depend upon its ability to manage internal conflict and disagreement that may arise. Once cooperative patterns of interaction are developed, the diversity of information and perspectives characteristic of the group can increase performance when the group is dealing with tasks that benefit from the consideration of multiple points of view.

In a 1993 study, Warren Watson, Kamalesh Kumar, and Larry Michaelsen reviewed the performance of thirty-six work groups composed of upper-level undergraduates from a large university in the southwestern United States.[11] Seventeen of the groups were homogeneous, and nineteen were diverse. All groups were given the same series of tasks across a period of slightly more than four months. The researchers found that initially the homogeneous groups scored higher than the diverse groups in terms of internal interaction processes and performance. In addition, both types of groups improved over time, but by the end of the period under analysis, the diverse groups outperformed the homogeneous groups in terms of the range of perspectives and alternatives considered in trying to solve a complex hypothetical problem.

To the extent that diversity leads to the better performance of work teams or more effective operations, it carries organizational benefits. In other contexts, additional benefits are derived for similar reasons. Within institutions of higher education, for example, substantial evidence exists that student-body diversity enhances the educational experience of all students, much as Justice Powell had argued in 1978 in the *Bakke* case *(Regents of the University of California v. Bakke)*. Some of the most thorough work documenting the educational benefits of student-body diversity is that by Patricia Gurin demonstrating a variety of positive educational outcomes associated with exposure to a multiplicity of ideas, perspectives, and beliefs characteristic of greater levels of diversity on campus.[12] In general, exposure to a variety of views allows students the opportunity to evaluate and assess their own perspectives and prepares them after graduation to deal effectively with diversity in an increasingly interconnected and diverse world. Gruin's work provided the basis for expert testimony in defense of the University of Michigan affirmative action programs challenged in the *Grutter (Grutter v. Bollinger et al.)* and *Gratz (Gratz v. Bollinger)* cases and, along with other similar research, helped to persuade the Supreme Court that achieving diversity within a student body was a compelling interest of state colleges and universities.[13] As integration is realized across employment and educational segments of society, proponents of affirmative action argue that core democratic values are enhanced. Democracy requires participation and inclusiveness, not only in the political process, but in all aspects of society. Democracy implies that all individuals and their views are valuable. According to this point of view, any efforts that promote inclusiveness, including affirmative action, also help to build a democratic culture.[14] Elizabeth Anderson has argued, for example, that the dismantling of barriers to opportunity, which have worked to the disadvantage of minority racial and ethnic groups and women, is essential for the promotion of a democratic civil society.[15] In the context of the government bureaucracy, democratic values enhanced by integration and inclusiveness are especially important. Efforts to combat discrimination and achieve integration within the public workforce also provide an example for the private sector. If the government cannot get its own house in order, how can it be expected to promote integration in the private sector?[16] In addition, when the public workforce is more representative of the people served, its diversity will help to ensure that all interests are represented in bureaucratic policymaking processes. This idea, known as representative bureaucracy, has spawned a significant literature within the academic field of public administration.[17] The concept of representative bureaucracy is salient because substantial power to shape or establish public policy rests in the hands of government employees. At the top of the public bureaucracy, of course, are elected officials, who are directly accountable to the people through the electoral process. Below them are political appointees who must answer to their elected superiors. Below the appointees, one finds the career or "permanent" bureaucracy staffed through civil service procedures. The civil service comprises the bulk of the public sector workforce, and in order to preserve politically neutral competence, its members are typically shielded from partisan removal. The necessities of modern government, however, mean that substantial power over the formation and implementation of public policy is exercised at the discretion of employees within the bureaucracy. Their expertise, coupled with the inability of political authorities to address the minutia of public programs, makes this situation unavoidable and desirable. Yet, at the same time, an accountability problem arises. The theory of representative bureaucracy posits that because bureaucrats (like all people) make decisions in part on the basis of personal values and per-ceptions—and because those values and perceptions are shaped by social-ization experiences that vary with race, ethnicity, and gender—diversity within the bureaucracy that produces a public workforce representative of the people in terms of such characteristics as race, ethnicity, and gender will help to ensure that all interests are represented when policy decisions are made.[18] Numerous empirical studies have tested this proposition and have found that the interests of minorities and women are more likely to be heard in policy processes when minorities and women are present in the organizations involved.[19] Affirmative action in higher education may also ultimately assist in the alleviation of a range of other social difficulties. Ar-eas with large minority populations have frequently suffered from a lack of physicians, nurses, lawyers, and other professionals. Efforts to increase minority representation within institutions of higher education, and es-pecially in professional degree programs in those schools, will increase the likelihood that more graduates of those programs will go to work in mi-nority communities where their services are often urgently needed.

To summarize, the arguments for affirmative action thus far rest on the view that justice is served when discrimination directed against minori-ties and women is overcome, and diversity, which is enhanced by efforts to combat discrimination, leads to the promotion of a wide range of benefits including such values as enhanced organizational effectiveness and broader accountability in government. Readers might ask, however, why a policy of strict enforcement of nondiscrimination law would not be sufficient to achieve those ends. Why are affirmative action programs necessary?

The Need for a Proactive Orientation

If the goal is to combat discrimination that has been directed historically toward minorities and women, why not simply rely on strict prohibitions of discrimination, as many political conservatives are arguing? Would such a policy succeed in overcoming discrimination and achieving the benefits of diversity? Perhaps it would, but proponents of affirmative action have argued that if that objective were reached through such an approach, the process would likely be a torturously slow one. History demonstrates that progress was painfully difficult when efforts rested primarily on attempts to investigate and resolve individual complaints of discrimination. In addition, such an approach places the burden of initiating action on the victims of discriminatory behavior, and experience has also shown that numerous reasons exist why victims may not always come forward readily with complaints. Furthermore, such an approach ignores the concept of compensatory justice—the idea that some effort must be made to affirmatively redress past or current inequities. A method is needed, according to this argument, which will allow elimination of discrimination by means more effective and timely than the investigation of individual complaints alone. Many believe affirmative action provides that method, and the policy was originally justified on those grounds.

Affirmative action's supporters believe that a policy of strict nondiscrimination will bring about the desired state of affairs much more gradually, if it does so at all, than will a program that is positive or proactive in orientation; and they might suggest considering parallel examples from the field of public health. Are such threats as tuberculosis or small pox best combated by simply reacting to individual cases when those who have been stricken bring their affliction to the attention of medical professionals and seek treatment? If all cases are found, and the treatment is successful, this strategy could eventually prove effective. But a better approach for public health would be to have society take the initiative by immunizing people from the disease. Scores of people are protected through such an approach. Suffering is ended much more rapidly. This type of approach is what affirmative action's advocates intended with regard to the problem of discrimination directed against racial minorities and women. From this perspective, justice delayed is, indeed, justice denied.

If this is so, however, then why not be content with the earliest forms of affirmative action based on outreach and recruitment efforts? Again, proponents will argue that the answer has to do with the need to deal with the problem of discrimination against minorities and women as expeditiously as possible. The presence of goals and timetables and the preferences they imply are expected to produce results more rapidly than earlier forms of affirmative action. Discrimination against minorities and women is often subtle and difficult to overcome, but, Bergmann, for example, has argued that goals energize.[20] They direct and spur action. Goals are used in virtually every area of managerial activity to stimulate movement, and they provide a standard against which progress can be measured. A certain amount of logic is inherent in the establishment of goals and the operation of preferences to achieve those goals if the object is to, within a reasonable period of time, bring minorities and women into positions from which they have typically been excluded. Proponents for affirmative action ask why assistance should be delayed for people who have been historically disadvantaged when presumably effective action is possible. Affirmative action's opponents will argue, however, that the issue is not quite so simple.

Arguments in Opposition to Preferential Affirmative Action

Because the focus of controversy over affirmative action has been on the use of racial-, ethnic-, and sex-based preferences since at least the early 1970s, the discussion here will concentrate on arguments raised in opposition to that approach. Proponents believe that limited preferences are necessary to overcome discrimination against minorities and women and achieve the advantages of diversity as rapidly as possible. A consideration of five key arguments from the point of view of those who oppose affirmative action will now be presented.

Argument One: Group-Based Preferences
Violate Core American Values

Perhaps the most basic argument against preferential forms of affirmative action is that such policies run counter to the widely shared American view that the individual is the relevant unit in society and that justice should be color (and usually sex) blind.[21] In other words, individuals should be evaluated, not groups, and they should be judged on the basis of their personal merits. Individuals are the victims of discrimination, and the right to be free from injustice must be affixed to them rather than to groups from which they may be drawn.[22] Importantly, in the analogy to runners discussed previously, the harm is borne by an identified individual. When such an individual victim is recognized, compensatory action is warranted. From this perspective, then, no preference should be given on the basis of group identity or other characteristics unrelated to an individual's qualifications. A policy of strict nondiscrimination, with selection based purely on qualifications, would be more desirable than one relying on racial or gender preferences. Self-reliance and individualism are principles by which our economy is organized and our citizenship is understood. Group-based preferences are anathema to those principles.[23] This line of argument is persuasive to many, but the defenders of affirmative action respond that history shows that groups, as well as individuals, are the targets of harmful activity. Violence directed toward individual members of specific racial groups, for example, has intimidated, threatened, and harmed all members of those groups, not just the individual victims of violence.[24] Indeed, the purpose of such violence has often been to threaten and suppress entire groups. When injury is directed toward people because of their membership in specified groups, as is the case with racial or gender discrimination, group-based remedies are considered by many to be appropriate.[25] In addition, David Skrentny suggests other inconsistencies in the argument against group-based preferences. Preferences are not opposed as a matter of principle according to Skrentny. In fact, preferences are applied in many situations to specific groups with few questions raised.[26] Veterans' preference in the selection of government employees is one example. Governments commonly add points to the civil service examination scores of veterans. The federal government, for example, adds five points to the scores of veterans who have served in specified conflicts involving combat and gives an absolute preference to qualified disabled veterans. These procedures have the effect of moving veterans up on the eligibility lists for public employment, yet they raise little or no controversy. Other preferential practices are also accepted without dispute. Business owners, for example, will make positions available for their children or other family members.[27] Elite colleges and universities give preference in admissions processes to children of substantial donors or influential alumni.[28] As Skrentny notes, when it comes to affirmative action, it may not be the preference as such that is objectionable, but the fact that it goes to minorities or women who are deemed less deserving of special consideration, despite the sacrifices they have made and often continue to make because of discrimination directed against them.[29] Despite these arguments, opponents of preferential affirmative action programs are steadfast in their belief that individuals should be judged only on the basis of their own abilities and talents. They should be permitted the opportunity to advance as far as those abilities and talents will carry them. To give special preference to some groups because members of those groups have suffered or continue to suffer injustice is, from this perspective, to substitute one form of inequity for another.

Argument Two: Preferences Often Benefit the Wrong People

The notion that individuals should be judged on their own merits also provides the foundation for an additional criticism of preferential affirmative action. The argument here is essentially that positions will go to the "wrong" individuals, a problem that can occur two ways. First, those who benefit from the affirmative action preference may not need the preference they receive. All members of minority groups or women, according to this argument, are not disadvantaged. This is essentially the argument Supreme Court Justice Clarence Thomas made when asked to explain his opposition to preferential affirmative action prior to his confirmation to the Court. Thomas responded by questioning why his son should receive preferential treatment, simply because he is African American, when he suffers no economic disadvantage.[30]

Supporters of affirmative action maintain, however, that this argument misconstrues the purpose of affirmative action, which is not primarily to benefit the particular individuals who receive help from the policy but, rather, to assist groups who have suffered discrimination. Should Justice Thomas' son receive preferential treatment? Proponents of affirmative action would answer yes, if his son seeks employment with an organization that had previously excluded African Americans or had a significant underrepresentation of African Americans in its workforce. Similarly, if he sought admission to a college or university in which African Americans were underrepresented, a preference might be defended from this point of view. Again, the preference is not designed to promote the selection of a particular individual. It is fashioned as a mechanism by which organizations, including those providing employment or higher education, change patterns of behavior that have previously operated to the disadvantage of minorities and women.

Nevertheless, many people have difficulty justifying advantages being given to individual minority group members or women who exhibit no signs of having been personally disadvantaged previously. They should be free to compete on an equal footing, according to this argument, but not placed ahead of others who may be just as deserving as they are. As time passes and greater measures of equity are achieved between racial and ethnic groups in society, this line of reasoning will be increasingly difficult to discredit.

The second way in which the "wrong" person may be advantaged by preferential affirmative action occurs, as critics are eager to point out, when a less qualified minority group member or woman receives a position instead of a more qualified white man. This is an issue that was addressed briefly in chapter I. The supposition is that positions should go only to the individuals most qualified, which does not always happen when affirmative action is practiced, and the result is organizational costs in efficiency and productivity or the admission of university students with lower ability. Affirmative action's proponents, however, raise the question as to whether, in the absence of preferential affirmative action, only the best qualified will be selected. To assume so may place too much faith in employers or other officials and assume too much from examinations or other screening devices. As previously acknowledged, business owners often practice nepotism when distributing high-level positions, and selective colleges and universities commonly have legacy programs for admission of the children of donors. Additionally, in the absence of affirmative action, job opportunities may be advertised in only a limited way that may not reach into minority communities. Training opportunities that build skill and experience necessary for advancement may not be equitably distributed.[31] Marc Bendick, Jr. provides an example of a warehouse where promotion to a position of full-time forklift operator required eight hours of prior experience in driving forklifts that was usually achieved by filling in for absent drivers. The foreman in charge of the warehouse favored white males for these temporary positions, and as a result, minorities and women were unable to gain sufficient experience necessary to "qualify" for promotion.[32] In the absence of affirmative action, minority or female employees could seek redress by lodging complaints with management, or perhaps with the federal Equal Employment Opportunity Commission (EEOC) assuming the warehouse was covered by nondiscrimination law. An EEOC complaint could take months for investigation, and in the end, litigation could be necessary to force the employer to change the practice, although that outcome would obviously not be guaranteed. An affirmative action program and good faith efforts to meet goals for minority and female employment as forklift operators would create an equitable distribution of those jobs much more expeditiously, proponents of such a policy would argue.

Difficulties in identifying the "most qualified" also become obvious when one considers that the examination or other mechanisms utilized to screen individuals for selection are often only imprecise predictors of future performance. Hiring and promotion decisions, for example, are frequently based on applicants' scores on written or unwritten performance examinations and interviews with supervisors. These measures may be generally related to job performance, and may clearly distinguish between those who are basically qualified and unqualified, but they cannot always validly or reliably make fine distinctions between individuals. The screening mechanisms themselves may not be bias-free nor are they free from the exercise of subjective judgment.

These difficulties were well illustrated in a reverse discrimination case from the 1980s in Santa Clara County, California.[33] The county's Public Works Department had an opening for a dispatcher's position. Among those who applied for the position were current employees Diane Joyce and Paul Johnson. As will be discussed more fully in chapter 5, their qualifications were evaluated through an interview process conducted by a panel of supervisors who assigned numerical scores to reflect their impressions of the candidate's abilities. Johnson was scored at 77, while Joyce received a 75. Johnson argued that his higher score suggested that he was better qualified for the promotion than was Joyce, but such a conclusion was not at all clear. Joyce, who admittedly was laboring in a male-dominated field, had previously experienced difficulties with at least one member of the interview panel who had refused to properly equip her for an earlier job assignment and had made derogatory comments about her based, in part, on sex. Internal observers are left to wonder who, between Johnson and Joyce, was actually better qualified. Both had met and exceeded the threshold of being minimally qualified, and affirmative action, when properly construed, provides preferences only for those who meet that standard. In compliance with the agency's affirmative action program, Joyce eventually got the promotion.

It remains possible, and perhaps even likely, however, that less qualified individuals will occasionally be preferred over those with better qualifications when affirmative action is implemented. Such a result will not always be avoidable. Opponents of such policies find that outcome unacceptable. The advocates for preferential affirmative action must be willing to accept this as one of the potential costs associated with the policy. However, following an extensive review of the economics literature on the impact of affirmative action, Harry Holzer and David Neumark found "very little compelling evidence of deleterious efficiency effects" of the policy that would be expected if affirmative action resulted in the employment of workers with generally lower qualifications.[34]

Argument Three: Affirmative Action Harms White Men

Some opponents of affirmative action argue that it makes victims of innocent nonminority men. From this perspective, not only will affirmative often operate to benefit the wrong individuals, it also places the cost of compensation for past or present discrimination on people who may have never been guilty of discrimination themselves. White men, opponents suggest, are unfairly harmed by affirmative action. It is, in effect, reverse discrimination. Instead of being allowed to compete fairly for employment or other valued positions, nonminority men suffer the disadvantage of competing against those who receive preferential consideration.

The argument for affirmative action relies in part on the assertion that to have a broader distribution of opportunities, the proportion of positions held by white men must decline. As society moves from a system that has worked to the advantage of white men, because of discrimination against minorities and women, to a system where minorities and women are granted a greater share of opportunity, opportunities for white men will be reduced. As noted in chapter 1 and earlier in this chapter, this is the redistributive nature of affirmative action. Proponents suggest that this propels society from a noncompetitive to a competitive system. White men as a consequence face a tougher contest for positions sought. As a group, white men may not fare as well as before because they have lost the competitive advantage historically enjoyed. From this perspective, affirmative action is not reverse discrimination. Stanley Fish has argued, for example, that "to equate the efforts to remedy the plight of racial minorities with the actions that produced it is to twist history."[35] Fish charges further that to suggest that affirmative action treats white men unfairly is to suggest that their situation is equal to that of minorities. Even so, opponents assert that nonminority men will not be judged solely on their own merits under affirmative action, but will be judged in part on the basis of their race or sex.

Argument Four: Affirmative Action Stigmatizes Its Beneficiaries

Affirmative action's opponents also suggest that the policy is undesirable because it unfairly stigmatizes minorities and women who benefit from its operation. The argument here is that many people will see the success of minority group members or women as coming only from affirmative action and will assume that in the absence of affirmative action they would not have received the jobs, promotions, or college seats awarded.[36] As a result, affirmative action's beneficiaries are considered unworthy. Because, from this view, minorities or women received their positions only due to race, ethnicity, or sex, they were unjustly selected. Indeed, in some instances, the beneficiaries of affirmative action themselves may be filled with self-doubt.

Do such individuals receive their positions merely because of race or sex? Affirmative action's supporters claim that if the policy is properly applied, the answer is no. Under those circumstances, preferences go only to those who are qualified. Does the possibility exist that some nonminority men were better qualified? Perhaps, but, again, the imprecise nature by which qualifications are often measured must be considered. Has affirmative action ever worked to the advantage of unqualified minorities or women? Undoubtedly it has, but the cure for that problem is to end those practices rather than to abandon affirmative action altogether, supporters suggest. Those who oppose the policy are not so optimistic. From their point of view, a preference for minority group members or women means, other things being equal, that selection will be determined by race, ethnicity, or sex.

Argument Five: Affirmative Action Is Not Needed

A final argument raised in opposition to affirmative action is that it is simply no longer needed. Given the advances that have been made for minorities and women, the argument goes, members of those groups are not nearly as disadvantaged as they have been in the past, and as a result, preferential practices cannot be defended on any grounds. As noted in chapter 1, Stephan and Abigail Thernstrom, among others, have made this point vigorously. If affirmative action is pursued, according to this line of thought, the policy will only work to the advantage of groups that no longer need it.

Backers of affirmative action will usually acknowledge that one day, hopefully, a point will be reached when such programs truly are no longer needed. The essential question, from their position, is whether that point has already been reached. Affirmative action is supported by its proponents as a way of increasing the representation of minorities and women in areas where they are underrepresented. When underrepresentation ends, affirmative action will no longer be justified. Of course, this raises the question of what standard of representation should be used. How should fair representation be defined? Clearly, such a standard should be based on a reasonable estimate of the availability of qualified minority or female applicants, since no case can be made for preferring people without requisite qualifications. But, if that is so, then the standard will vary depending on the type of positions at issue. In the employment context, for example, the federal government has a broader array of positions, and more of them, than any other organization in the United States. In the early 1970s, when preferential affirmative action in the form of goals and timetables first came to the federal civil service, African Americans were not underrepresented in the government work force overall. In 1971, for example, they held 11.3 percent of all general schedule and equivalent jobs. The problem was that their jobs were found primarily in the lower levels of the federal bureaucracy. African Americans comprised nearly 22 percent of the work force in federal employment grades 1–4, but held only approximately 3 percent of the positions in grades 12–18 at that time.[37] Since then, significant progress has been made. As of 2005, the African American share of positions in the Senior Executive Service (SES), the top positions in the government that had earlier consisted primarily of grades 16–18, stands at 8.4 percent. As a result, underrepresentation, even at this highest level, has been significantly reduced, although the African American proportion of the national population stands at approximately 13 percent, and the African American proportion of students enrolled in colleges and universities nationwide is approximately 12 percent. Nevertheless, African American representation in some federal departments and agencies remains very low. Only 2.8 percent of the SES employees of the Department of the Navy are black, for example, and African American representation stands at only 1.5 percent in the Department of State. Other departments within the defense establishment have only between 2.0 and 3.6 percent of their SES workforces filled by African Americans.[38] Other examples like this abound, suggesting that although much has been accomplished to overcome the underrepresentation of African Americans, areas where representation is likely to remain below reasonable estimates of parity still exist. In those circumstances, proponents of affirmative action would argue, a qualified African American who applies for a position should receive some preference for employment. If such situations are fewer in 2005 than they were thirty years ago, that is good news from their perspective. Affirmative action may be justified less frequently than before, but still, in areas where underrepresentation persists, preferential affirmative action may be necessary. Discrimination against minorities and women has not been completely eradicated, according to supporters of affirmative action. Bergman and others have argued that discrimination has proved to be a tenacious foe.[39] They are not surprised to find organizations or units within organizations where the representation of minorities or women is below expectations given reasonable estimates of the availability of qualified applicants from those groups. Opponents counter that the progress that has been made in the past thirty years has substantially undermined the need for a continuation of the policy.

Conclusion

Affirmative action has stirred significant controversy, and it continues to do so. This controversy is likely to exist as long as preferential forms of the policy continue to be practiced. Strong arguments are raised on both sides of the issue. Affirmative action is an area of public policy that provides no simple or easy answers. Proponents see affirmative action as a way of rooting out the vestiges of discrimination that have suppressed members of racial and ethnic minority groups and women for centuries. Opponents see it as an unjustified violation of the concept of equality of opportunity; they argue that affirmative action should be ended and replaced with a policy grounded firmly on the principle of nondiscrimination. Given that jobs, careers, and educational or business opportunities are at stake, this dispute is not unexpected. Nor is it surprising that most of those who oppose preferential affirmative action are drawn from among those who have usually benefited without it. Ultimately, the debate will end when discrimination against minorities and women has been overcome to such an extent that under-representation is difficult, if not impossible, to find. Perhaps one day that goal will be obtained, but in the interim, the argument continues, and much of it takes place within our judicial system. A consideration of the role of the courts in establishing the legal boundaries for preferential affirmative action, and in particular, the cases that have come before the U.S. Supreme Court comprise the subject matter for the next chapter.

five

The Supreme Court and Affirmative Action

An Examination of the Early Development of Statutory and Constitutional Constraints

As was discussed in previous chapters, by the late 1960s and early 1970s, race and gender-conscious approaches to affirmative action had come into frequent use in the struggle to overcome discrimination against minorities and women. Numerical goals and timetables were often developed, and limited preferences for women and members of minority groups were established in many organizations. Precisely because these actions are premised on racial or gender distinctions, they present a challenge to the doctrine of strict nondiscrimination and have given rise to significant controversy. As formerly noted, a fundamental conflict between core values embracing social equity on the one hand and individual rights on the other is at issue.[1]

The task of adjudicating disputes arising out of the application of racial or gender-based preferences incorporated within affirmative action programs rests, of course, with the courts and ultimately with the Supreme Court. This chapter reviews court rulings on preferential affirmative action in order to identify the legal boundaries of such programs for government and private-sector organizations. Because the issue is so divisive and because it touches on such a broad range of opportunities in employment and education, careful consideration of limitations placed by the courts on affirmative action is essential. The central question is, given the decisions that have been issued, Where do we now stand with respect to the legal permissibility of affirmative action?

To begin this discussion, readers should note that from a legal perspective preferential affirmative action arises in three ways. It may be the result of a direct court order, it may arise as part of a consent decree sanctioned by a court to settle litigation, or it may be voluntarily adopted by an organization. Affirmative action required by court order is authorized by the 1964 Civil Rights Act, although the act does not specifically describe the kinds of preferential programs that have often been developed, and it requires that a finding of discrimination be made before a court may order an affirmative action remedy. Standards for the review of court-ordered preferential affirmative action were articulated by the Supreme Court in 1984 and 1987 in *Firefighters Local v. Stotts* and *United States v. Paradise*.[2] Guidelines for permissible preferential affirmative action embodied in consent decrees are quite similar to those for voluntary affirmative action and were outlined in 1986 in *Firefighters v. City of Cleveland*.[3] Voluntary affirmative action, consisting of race- or sex-conscious practices established by an organization without external persuasion or compulsion arising out of litigation, includes preferential programs freely adopted, such as legislation that sets aside a certain portion of government contracting dollars for minority contractors, regulations that require government contractors to establish goals for the employment of specified numbers of minorities or women, or affirmative action programs that grant limited preferences to minorities and women in employment or admission to institutions of higher education. Because most affirmative action is "voluntary," in the sense that the term is used here, this approach is the focus of concern in this chapter.[4] Through a detailed review of Supreme Court decisions, the legal boundaries of voluntary affirmative action by public and private organizations will be elaborated. The objective is to clarify what organizations may do with regard to affirmative action and what they may not do.

Statutory and Constitutional Constraints on Affirmative Action: The Earliest Cases

Racial and sexual distinctions drawn between individuals by governmental or private organizations for purposes of employment and incorporated into affirmative action plans are governed by Title VII of the Civil Rights Act of 1964 as amended by the Equal Employment Opportunity Act of 1972 and the Civil Rights Act of 1991. Sections 703 and 717 of Title VII define as unlawful any employment practice that discriminates against any individual on account of race, color, religion, sex, or national origin.[5] Similarly, Title VI of the Civil Rights Act of 1964 prohibits discrimination on the basis of race, ethnicity, or sex by any organization, including colleges and universities, receiving federal financial assistance. Thus, as noted in chapter 1, race- or sex-based preferences implemented by private or public institutions will need to be reconciled with Title VI or Title VII prohibitions on discrimination.

In addition to these specific statutory constraints, however, *government* organizations also face restrictions on affirmative action imposed by the Equal Protection Clause of the U.S. Constitution's Fourteenth Amendment and the due process clause of the Fifth Amendment. The equal protection clause forbids states from denying to any person within their jurisdictions the "equal protection of the laws." Distinctions established by states and their local subdivisions on the basis of race or sex (including such distinctions incorporated into affirmative action plans) could presumably constitute a denial of equal protection. Because the Fourteenth Amendment applies only to actions of the states, however, its restrictions do not limit the federal government. The due process clause of the Fifth Amendment governs affirmative action by the federal government inasmuch as it has been interpreted by the Supreme Court as requiring equal protection of the laws.[6]

Given the restrictions on discrimination imposed by the 1964 Civil Rights Act as amended and the Fifth and Fourteenth Amendments to the Constitution, how is it that race- or sex-conscious affirmative action that on its face grants limited preferences to selected minorities and women is legally permissible? The answer rests on judicial interpretation of the particular affirmative action practices in place and the meaning of the relevant statutory and constitutional constraints as viewed by the courts.

Statutory Limitations on Affirmative Action

The Supreme Court has held that violations of Title VII occur in two ways. One method of violation is known as disparate impact. As discussed in chapter 2, the concept of disparate impact, as originally articulated by the Supreme Court in 1971 in *Griggs et al. v. Duke Power Company*, holds that employment practices that on their face are nondiscriminatory may still be in violation of Title VII if they have the effect of classifying employees on racial, sexual, or other prohibited grounds. The second manner in which violations of Title VII may occur is known as disparate treatment. Disparate treatment means that an employer purposely engages in prohibited employment practices because of their discriminatory effect. In other words, the employer intentionally and openly engages in discrimination on the basis of race, color, religion, sex, or national origin.

Race or sex preferences within employment-related affirmative action plans represent practices that purposefully classify applicants or employees on the basis of race and sex. When challenged in court under Title VII, such practices fall within the analytical framework required in disparate treatment cases. In such litigation, once the case has been made that race or sex has been taken into account in employment decisions, the employer may defend those actions by articulating a legitimate nondiscriminatory reason for the decisions, just as they would in any other discrimination case. In 1979 in an important decision in *United Steelworkers of America v. Weber,* the Court held that the elimination of racial imbalances in traditionally segregated job categories provides such a reason, because such action is consistent with Title VII's objective of "break[ing] down old patterns of racial segregation and hierarchy."[7]

Weber was the first case before the Supreme Court challenging the Title VII legality of race-conscious affirmative action in employment. The case involved a voluntary affirmative action plan negotiated as part of a collective bargaining agreement between Kaiser Aluminum and Chemical Corporation and the United Steelworkers of America. The plan reserved for blacks 50 percent of the openings in an in-plant craft training program until the black proportion of craft workers in the plant approximated the proportion of blacks in the local labor force. The Supreme Court upheld the legality of the affirmative action plan arguing that although Title VII, as indicated in Section 703, cannot be interpreted as requiring preferential treatment to overcome a racial imbalance, it does not preclude voluntary efforts to overcome such an imbalance. In view of the legislative history and purposes of Title VII, the Court held that the prohibition on discrimination could not be read literally to proscribe all race-conscious affirmative action plans. Writing for a majority of the Court, Justice Brennan noted that if Congress had meant to prohibit all race-conscious affirmative action, it easily could have done so "by providing that Title VII would not require or *permit* racially preferential integration efforts."[8] One might also reason, although Brennan did not articulate this argument, that if it was clear that voluntary affirmative action involving limited racial preferences was prohibited by the statute, then it would not have been necessary for Congress to indicate that such action was not required. The plan at issue in *Weber* was found to be permissible under Title VII because it conformed to the following limitations: (1) The plan was designed to correct a racial imbalance caused by a tradition of segregation in the positions at issue. (2) The plan did not unnecessarily trammel the interests of white employees since it did not require the discharge of white workers and their replacement with black workers; nor did the plan create an absolute bar to the advancement of white employees since half of the positions in the training program were reserved for whites. (3) The plan was a temporary measure not designed to maintain a racial balance once the immediate imbalance was eliminated.

Because *Weber* addressed the legality of voluntary affirmative action by a private employer, the question remained as to whether its outcome would guide the statutory review of voluntary affirmative action undertaken by a public employer. This question was not definitively settled until 1987 in the decision in *Johnson v. Transportation Agency, Santa Clara County, California.*[9] In *Johnson,* the Court applied the criteria outlined in *Weber* to a voluntary race and sex-conscious affirmative action plan adopted by the Transportation Agency of Santa Clara County, California. The affirmative action plan provided that in making employment decisions within traditionally segregated job classifications where women or minorities were significantly underrepresented, the Transportation Agency could consider the sex or race of a job candidate along with the individual's qualifications. No specific numbers of positions were set aside for minorities or women, but the eventual objective was to have minorities and women employed in positions roughly in proportion to their representation in the relevant local labor force. Paul Johnson, a male employee of the Transportation Agency, brought suit alleging the plan violated Title VII when, despite the fact that both he and a female employee were essentially equally qualified, the woman received the promotion at issue once sex was taken into account. Johnson initially won in district court, but that decision was overturned by the circuit court of appeals. The Supreme Court, following the *Weber* precedent, affirmed the circuit court decision. The affirmative action plan did not violate Title VII.

With the announcement of the *Johnson* decision, a relatively clear set of standards emerged for judging the *statutory* legality of voluntary race or gender-conscious affirmative action programs by government or private employers.[10] When challenged under Title VII, such programs must meet the following limitations:

1. Affirmative action must be targeted to address a manifest racial or gender imbalance in traditionally segregated job categories. Proof of prior discrimination by the employer, however, is not necessary. Nor is it necessary that a manifest imbalance be such that it would support a *prima facie* case of discrimination against the employer. Furthermore, when determining whether a manifest racial or gender imbalance exists, the employer must consider the proportion of minorities or women in traditionally segregated positions relative to the proportion of minorities or women with the requisite qualifications in the local labor force.

2. An affirmative action plan must not trammel the rights of nonminorities or men by requiring their discharge and replacement with minorities or women or by creating an absolute bar to their advancement. In addition, race or gender may not be the only factors considered in the selection process. The qualifications of applicants for position at issue must be considered. No preferences for unqualified individuals are allowed.

3. Affirmative action must be constructed as a temporary strategy. Once a racial or gender imbalance is corrected, affirmative action can no longer be justified as a method of maintaining a given balance.

Constitutional Limitations on Affirmative Action

Although the *Johnson* decision indicates that in specified circumstances voluntary race or sex-based preferences in affirmative action by a public employer will withstand statutory challenges, constitutional issues remain. In most instances, the courts apply one of two analytical standards when deciding whether government actions that create classifications among people violate the equal protection components of the Fifth or Fourteenth Amendments. The first standard simply requires that a rational basis exist for the distinctions drawn between individuals. More specifically, a rational relationship must be present between the distinctions imposed and a legitimate governmental end. A state requirement that public school teachers hold college degrees and state certification meets this standard of review because presumably a rational association exists between that requirement and the legitimate state objective of ensuring that teachers are relatively competent.[11] Under the rational-basis standard, the burden of proof rests with those challenging the governmental classification, that is, plaintiffs bear the burden of showing that the challenged government action serves no legitimate governmental purpose or, if a legitimate purpose exists, the classification is not rationally related to its achievement. This standard is applied in the review of distinctions such as those associated with business regulation or licensing or other forms of economic or social regulation that do not involve issues of race or fundamental rights.[12]

When government classifications limit fundamental freedoms or rights or force distinctions based on race or national origin, however, the second major standard requiring a heightened level of scrutiny, commonly known as strict scrutiny, has usually been applied. Under the application of strict scrutiny, the government must defend the validity of classifications created by demonstrating that they serve a compelling governmental interest and are narrowly tailored to meet that interest. There must be no alternatives for achieving the government interest that are less restrictive on the interests or rights of parties who may be impacted by the classifications.

As a consequence, laws reviewed under strict scrutiny are more vulnerable than laws merely subjected to the rational-basis standard.

When classifications involve sex-based distinctions, a middle ground between the rational-basis standard and strict scrutiny is reached. The Court has considered sex-based distinctions "quasi-suspect" because, from the Court's view, there may be common instances where distinctions between the sexes are legitimate. As a result, an intermediate level of review, requiring that classifications be substantially related to important governmental objectives, is usually applied to classifications based on sex.[13] Interestingly, the Court has never explicitly addressed the constitutionality of sex-based distinctions in the context of affirmative action because a case properly framing that issue has yet to come before the Court.

Despite the general analytical framework developed for equal protection review, the Supreme Court has struggled to determine the appropriate level of review for race-based preferences in affirmative action programs. Race-based preferential affirmative action obviously draws distinctions in terms of race, and for that reason, some members of the Court have held that such programs must be subjected to strict scrutiny when challenged on constitutional grounds. Other justices, however, have held that the intermediate level of review requiring that such distinctions be substantially related to important (rather than compelling) governmental interests is the appropriate standard because the classifications in affirmative action are essentially benign.

This constitutional debate first emerged in the context of a Supreme Court decision on affirmative action in the case of *Regents of the University of California v. Bakke* in 1978.[14] In that case, an affirmative action admissions program at the medical school of the University of California at Davis was challenged under the Fourteenth Amendment (as well as Title VI of the 1964 Civil Rights Act) because the program provided for a special admissions procedure for members of minority groups by setting aside sixteen positions out of one hundred in the entering class for minority applicants. Alan Bakke, a white applicant who was denied admission while African-American applicants with lower qualifications (as measured by the University) were admitted, initiated the lawsuit.

The Supreme Court failed to reach a majority opinion except on the point that Bakke should be admitted. On the constitutional issue, four justices including Brennan, Marshall, White, and Blackmun argued that the medical school's program should be subjected only to intermediate scrutiny and that under that standard the program would be constitutional because it was substantially related to the important government interest of achieving a diverse student enrollment. In another opinion, Justices Stevens, Burger, Stewart, and Rehnquist found that the program was impermissible because it was inconsistent with Title VI. Finally, in a separate opinion, Justice Powell argued that strict scrutiny was the proper standard of constitutional review, and that under that standard, the program could not survive. Powell suggested, however, that race could be considered a factor in the admissions process at a public university to achieve diversity among students. He therefore agreed with Brennan, Marshall, White, and Blackmun that the state court's injunction prohibiting any use of race whatsoever should be overturned. According to Powell, student enrollment diversity was a sufficiently compelling interest to permit preferential affirmative action, but he concluded that race could not be the only factor considered. A school could not operate a racial quota system as, in his view, had been the case at the medical school at Davis. In other words, although Powell thought the Davis program served a compelling government interest, it was not narrowly tailored in that some seats in the entering class (the sixteen reserved for minorities) were not open to competition from all applicants.

The next case challenging the constitutionality of race-conscious affirmative action involved a program initiated by the federal government, and as it turned out, the intermediate standard of review prevailed. The case was *Fullilove v. Klutznick,* decided in 1980. The issue in *Fullilove* was the legality of a minority business enterprise set-aside provision of the federal Public Works Employment Act of 1977. This program required that at least 10 percent of federal funds distributed under the public works act was to be used to purchase services or supplies from minority-owned contractors or subcontractors. The set-aside provision was challenged for allegedly violating the equal protection component of the due process clause of the Fifth Amendment. The district court, the court of appeals, and the Supreme Court upheld the provision.

In its ruling, the Supreme Court established first that the minority business enterprise program fell within the scope of Congress' spending power, its authority to regulate commerce, and its authority under Section 5 of the Fourteenth Amendment. The Court argued also that appropriate deference should be given to an act of Congress established under legitimate authority. The Court then noted that the program was premised on a finding by Congress that in the past nonminority businesses had gained an unfair competitive advantage over minority firms because of discrimination in the distribution of federal contracting opportunities. Once this was established, the Court determined that racial classifications contained in the contested program served the important governmental interest of correcting past discrimination against minority contractors, that the program was substantially related to achieving that interest, and that it placed no undue burden on nonminority firms. The Court's deference to Congress as a coequal branch of the federal government acting under legitimate authority was of paramount importance in determining the outcome of the case.

In subsequent cases, however, affirmative action by state or local government employers was not granted the same deference as programs enacted by Congress. Consequently, constitutional limitations on state or local government efforts were more stringent than those applied initially to the federal level. Those limitations on state or local programs were first articulated in 1986 in *Wygant v. Jackson Board of Education*.[15] That case involved a collective bargaining agreement, negotiated between a school board and a teachers' union, providing for a seniority-based layoff procedure with an affirmative action component specifying that layoffs of minority personnel could at no time reduce the minority employment percentage below the level achieved prior to layoffs. In practice, this provision resulted in some nonminority teachers with seniority losing their jobs while less senior minority teachers were retained. The school board defended the policy as a means of correcting patterns of societal discrimination and helping to ensure that minority teachers would be present as role models for minority students. The policy was challenged under the equal protection clause of the Fourteenth Amendment.

The Supreme Court rejected the school board's arguments and found the affirmative action provision to be in violation of the Constitution, but the opinion of the Court was not uniform with regard to the appropriate standard of review. Chief Justice Burger and Justices Powell, Rehnquist, and O'Connor held that state actions establishing racial classifications must be subjected to strict scrutiny when reviewed under the Fourteenth Amendment. Justice White concurred in the judgment but did not explicitly address the issue of the appropriate standard of review. The plurality held, however, that state-imposed racial classifications must serve a compelling governmental interest and must be narrowly tailored. The school board's claim of societal discrimination as a basis for the affirmative action at issue was not considered sufficiently compelling for state or local action. Those in the plurality argued that evidence of prior discrimination by the government was necessary for an affirmative action provision to survive strict scrutiny, but the level of evidence of past discrimination necessary to justify racial preferences in affirmative action by a state or local employer was not definitively established. Justice O'Connor suggested that a statistical disparity adequate to support a *prima facie* case against the employer under Title VII would provide sufficient evidence. Justice White, however, found no justification adequate for the particular affirmative action plan at issue.

Nevertheless, societal discrimination alone would not provide an adequate basis for affirmative action under the Fourteenth Amendment.[16] The school board's justification based on its role model theory was also rejected as too "amorphous" a basis for imposing race relief.[17] Consequently, the school board failed to establish an adequate factual predicate for the affirmative action plan under review. Had the plan actually served a compelling interest, however, it still may not have been upheld since a majority of the justices would have in all likelihood found that the plan was not narrowly tailored. Chief Justice Burger and Justices Powell, Rehnquist, and O'Connor made this point specifically, and nothing in White's opinion leads to the conclusion that he would have considered the program narrowly tailored. Justice White stated in his decision that "[w]hatever the legitimacy of hiring goals or quotas may be, the discharge of white teachers to make room for blacks, none of whom has been shown to be a victim of any racial discrimination, is quite a different matter."[18] Chief Justice Burger and Justices Powell and Rehnquist had argued forcefully that the use of hiring goals would have provided a less intrusive means of promoting minority employment than the layoff provision of the affirmative action program at issue. As stated by Justice Powell, "[t]hough hiring goals may burden some individuals, they simply do not impose the same kind of injury that layoffs impose."[19]

Because only three Justices (Marshall, Brennan, and Blackmun) could be counted as unambiguous advocates of the intermediate level of scrutiny, *Wygant* established, for all practical purposes, that affirmative action by state or local governments would have to survive strict scrutiny.[20] Much of the ambiguity regarding Justice White's evolving position on the appropriate standard of constitutional review of affirmative action was clarified the following year. In *United States v. Paradise* (1987) Justice White, in a dissenting statement, aligned himself with the interpretation of strict scrutiny advocated by Justice O'Connor, Chief Justice Rehnquist, and Justice Scalia. In that case, the Court upheld affirmative action ordered by a District Court to increase black representation among Alabama state troopers at and above the rank of corporal. Justices O'Connor, Rehnquist, and Scalia dissented and argued that the affirmative action order would not survive strict scrutiny.

From the *Bakke, Fullilove, Wygant,* and *Paradise* decisions, the fundamental standards for constitutional review of race-conscious affirmative action in the mid to late 1980s may be discerned. Voluntary action by a state or local employer would, as a practical matter, have to survive strict scrutiny to ensure a favorable judicial response. Federal programs challenged under the Fifth Amendment's equal protection component would be held to the intermediate level of review. The major components of the standards that were articulated at this time can be presented as follows:

1. To achieve constitutional legitimacy, racial classifications incorporated into voluntary affirmative action programs by state or local employers were required to serve a compelling governmental interest. The correction of past discrimination by the government employer involved would likely be one such compelling interest. Statistical disparity sufficient to prove a *prima facie* Title VII case of disparate impact against the employer would probably suffice as adequate evidence of past discrimination. Societal discrimination alone was not a sufficient cause for a race-conscious program by a state or local government.
2. Once a compelling governmental interest was identified by a state or local government, the method used to achieve that interest had to be narrowly tailored. This means that affirmative action could not impose any undue burden on innocent third parties, that is, the government must use the least restrictive or intrusive means available to

achieve its end. Affirmative action that compromised a bona fide seniority system during times of layoffs, for example, would not withstand constitutional scrutiny because it placed an undue burden on nonminorities. Affirmative action in the form of hiring or promotion goals and timetables would be less intrusive than a program that violated seniority rights, and given evidence of past discrimination by the government, such an approach would presumably be acceptable.

3. Actions by the federal government taken pursuant to a legitimate act of Congress were held to a less restrictive standard of review that did not require specific findings of discrimination committed by the government. This standard required simply that the classifications at issue serve an important governmental interest and that they be substantially related to achievement of that interest. In essence, the Court determined that Congress had the power to require race-conscious remedies if they are substantially related to a redress of societal discrimination.[21]

Taking a Step Back? A Look at Three Cases from 1989

In 1989, the Supreme Court issued a number of decisions that were collectively perceived as signaling a retreat from the concept of affirmative action. The opinion delivered on January 23, 1989, in *City of Richmond v. J.A. Croson Co.* was seen by many as an attempt to place new limits on the ability of state and local governments to establish minority business enterprise contracting set-asides.[22] At least two additional cases decided later that year, *Wards Cove Packing Company v. Atonio* (decided June 5) and *Martin v. Wilks* (decided June 12), were also considered by proponents of affirmative action as causing major damage to progress achieved in the field of civil rights.[23] While such perceptions were not entirely unfounded, the direct implications of these cases for affirmative action were limited.

In the *Croson* decision, the Supreme Court reviewed a minority business enterprise set-aside program in Richmond, Virginia, that required city contractors to subcontract at least 30 percent of the dollar value they received to minority-owned businesses. The plan allowed for the waiver of the 30 percent set-aside if qualified minority business enterprises were unavailable or unable to participate. The J.A. Croson Company, an Ohio-based plumbing and heating contractor and the sole bidder on a contract to install plumbing in the city jail, applied for a waiver after experiencing difficulty in finding a qualified minority business willing to participate in the plumbing project. The city denied the waiver, and the Croson Company was denied the contract. Croson brought suit alleging that the set-aside plan was unconstitutional under the Fourteenth Amendment's equal protection clause.

The Federal District Court that tried the case upheld the affirmative action set-aside provision, and the Court of Appeals affirmed the District Court's decision. The Supreme Court vacated those lower court decisions and remanded the case for further consideration in light of its opinion in *Wygant*. On remand, the Court of Appeals found the set-aside program to be in violation of the Fourteenth Amendment. The Supreme Court subsequently affirmed that decision after applying the standard for constitutional review of race-conscious affirmative action articulated in the principal opinion in *Wygant*. No restrictive changes were made in the standard derived from the *Wygant* decision, however. In fact, a majority of the Court explicitly affirmed that standard. Consequently, *Croson*, imposed no new or increased constitutional requirements on state or local government affirmative action beyond those established by *Wygant*.[24]

The *Croson* Court found that the Richmond plan was not justified by a compelling governmental interest since no evidence had been presented sufficiently documenting past discrimination by the city in awarding construction contracts. To justify its program, the city had relied on statistical evidence of a disparity between the percentage of contracts awarded to minority businesses and the size of the city's minority population. The Court noted that the proper comparison would have been between the percentage of qualified minority businesses in the relevant labor market and the percentage of total city construction dollars awarded to minority contractors. The Court also found that the city's plan was not narrowly tailored, arguing, among other things, that the 30 percent set-aside was not sufficiently flexible and exhibited no relationship to the percentage of minority businesses qualified as potential contractors. Thus, had the city demonstrated a sufficient factual predicate for race-conscious affirmative action, the plan at issue would still have been invalidated.

In a strongly worded dissent from the *Croson* decision, Justice Marshall argued that the intermediate standard of review (rather than strict scrutiny) was the appropriate basis for constitutional consideration of benign racial classifications characteristic of affirmative action. Marshall suggested that more than sufficient evidence of past discrimination in the city of Richmond existed to justify the affirmative action set-aside under the intermediate standard. He also argued that the goal of 30 percent minority participation was appropriate. Marshall stressed that *Croson* was the first case in which a majority of the Court "adopted strict scrutiny as its standard of Equal Protection Clause review of race-conscious remedial measures."[25]

With respect to *Wards Cove*, the second of the 1989 decisions reviewed here, affirmative action was not at issue, so the standards for judicial review of voluntary affirmative action were not altered or even addressed. As a result, *Wards Cove* introduced no new restrictions on the legality of race- or gender-conscious affirmative action. The case did, however, have an important effect: it made it more difficult for minority litigants to prevail in Title VII disparate impact cases.

In *Wards Cove*, minority employees of two companies operating salmon canneries in Alaska brought suit, charging that employment practices at the canneries constituted impermissible racial discrimination and violated Title VII. The employees' claim was based on disparate impact theory and pointed to the employment of minorities almost exclusively in low-paying, unskilled cannery jobs that primarily involved cleaning and processing salmon, while noncannery jobs requiring higher skill levels were filled predominantly with nonminority personnel.

The Supreme Court rejected the minority employees' claim, noting that a comparison of the percentage of cannery workers who are minorities to the percentage of noncannery workers who are minorities does not establish a *prima facie* case of disparate impact. The proper comparison would be between the representation of minorities in the contested noncannery jobs and the proportion of minorities in the relevant labor force with skills that qualify them for such positions. In addition, the Court held that the employees must point to specific employment practices responsible for any disparate impact eventually demonstrated. Once a case for disparate impact is established, the employer may defend challenged employment practices by demonstrating that they serve a legitimate business purpose. However, contrary to previous interpretations, the employer need not prove that a business purpose is served by the contested practices.[26] Justice

White, writing for a majority of the Court, argued that the burden of proof remains with employees at all times to demonstrate that challenged employment practices are selected precisely because of their discriminatory effect. According to Justice White, in a disparate impact case, the employee "must prove that it was 'because of such individual's race, color,' etc. that he was denied a desired employment opportunity."[27]

The result was a situation in which potential minority plaintiffs would have to show that employers had intentionally engaged in discrimination if they were to prevail in disparate impact cases. Previously, as the dissenting justices in *Wards Cove* noted, intent had no place in disparate impact analysis. Disparate impact was considered to have occurred when personnel procedures that were neutral on their face and neutral in intent had a discriminatory impact, and no business justification for the procedures existed. However, following *Wards Cove*, the distinction between disparate impact and disparate treatment (i.e., intentional discrimination) appeared to turn solely on the issue of whether the procedure is facially neutral. This development was a "[departure] from the body of law engendered by [the] disparate impact theory" of discrimination outlined in *Griggs*.[28]

The last case considered here is *Martin v. Wilks*.[29] In that case Robert Wilks and six other white firefighters in Birmingham, Alabama, brought a suit under Title VII charging that because of affirmative action, they had been denied promotions in favor of less-qualified black firefighters. The city had promoted black firefighters pursuant to an affirmative action plan established by consent decrees entered in 1974 in response to an earlier suit by blacks. Wilks and the other white litigants were not parties to the consent decrees. The question that ultimately came before the Supreme Court was whether the challenge brought by Wilks and the other white employees constituted an impermissible collateral attack upon an established decree.

As noted earlier, consent decrees are voluntary settlements of legal disputes sanctioned by the Court. Under a consent decree, both parties in effect acknowledge that the settlement reflects a just determination of their rights, and the decision is binding on the consenting parties. Procedural rules exist for incorporating other parties into the settlement, and individuals who are not parties to a consent decree are not ordinarily bound by its terms. However, some federal courts have precluded nonparties that failed to intervene in a timely fashion from challenging consent decrees in Title VII cases. The preclusion of collateral attacks has been justified in part on the belief that it will promote voluntary settlement of Title VII lawsuits. The reasoning is that parties would have little incentive for settling Title VII suits through consent decrees if such decrees could later be challenged by those who do not join in the settlement.[30]

In *Martin v. Wilks*, the Supreme Court rejected the doctrine that made collateral attacks on consent decrees in Title VII cases impermissible. Justice Rehnquist, in delivering the opinion of the Court, argued that "[a] voluntary settlement in the form of a consent decree between one group of employees and their employer cannot possibly 'settle,' voluntarily or otherwise, the conflicting claims of another group of employees who do not join in the agreement."[31] In effect, nonparties to consent decrees are entitled to bring their claims to court.[32] The implication is that affirmative action established by consent decree will be more easily subject to challenge by nonminority employees. The allegations of such employees will be judged on their merits, however, and nothing in the *Martin* decision altered the standards by which affirmative action is justified under Title VII, either through a consent decree or through a voluntary effort without judicial involvement.

In summary, the most widely noted civil rights decisions by the Supreme Court in 1989 did not narrow the range of permissibility of voluntary affirmative action. Precedents established by *Weber, Johnson, Fullilove,* and *Wygant* remained in place. In fact, the 1990 decision in *Metro Broadcasting, Inc. v. Federal Communications Commission* reaffirmed the standard of analysis for federal affirmative action applied in *Fullilove*. In *Metro Broadcasting*, the Court upheld minority preference policies of the Federal Communications Commission that, among other things, allowed the consideration of race in the review of applications for radio and television broadcasting licenses. Because the program was sanctioned by Congress, was found to serve an important governmental interest, and was substantially related to achieving that interest, the minority preferences were upheld. In delivering the opinion of the Court, Justice Brennan stressed that nothing in the *Croson* decision can be read as restricting the precedent established by *Fullilove*.[33]

However, because *Croson* affirmed the standard developed in *Wygant* as the appropriate basis for constitutional review of voluntary affirmative

action by a state or local government, those governments who had wrong-
ly assumed *Fullilove* would control state or local minority business enterprise set-aside programs would have to review their efforts to be sure they
would survive strict scrutiny. In the period following *Croson*, a number of
state and local organizations were required to revise or abandon particular affirmative action practices.[34] Furthermore, the outcome of *Martin v.
Wilks* could reduce the willingness of public employers to enter into consent decrees requiring affirmative action if they believe such decrees will be
challenged by nonminority litigants. The shifting of the burden of proof
in disparate impact cases as required in *Wards Cove* may have also led some
employers to feel less pressure for affirmative action since it is was more difficult for minorities and women to prevail in discrimination suits. Thus,
impacts of *Croson, Martin v. Wilks*, and *Wards Cove* could have had a "chilling
effect" on affirmative action. Nevertheless, the legal basis for voluntary racial or sex-conscious affirmative action in the public sector was not eroded. The statutory and constitutional bases for affirmative action were left
intact. Two years later, in the Civil Rights Act of 1991, Congress amended
Title VII of the 1964 Civil Rights Act to, among other things, specifically re-
establish the operation of the burden of proof in disparate impact cases as
it had been originally articulated in 1971 in *Griggs*. Thus, the impact of *Wards
Cove* was short-lived. The more permissive view of federal affirmative action (as opposed to state or local affirmative action programs) that was the
legacy of *Fullilove, Wygant, Croson*, and *Metro Broadcasting*, however, would not
endure. That change, and other developments, are reviewed in chapter 6.

six

Cases from 1995 to 2003
Challenges, Uncertainty, and the Survival of Affirmative Action

In the 1995 case of *Adarand Constructors v. Federico Pena, Secretary of Transportation et al.*, the Supreme Court abandoned the distinction that had been made previously between federal government affirmative action and state or local government affirmative action.[1] The Court ruled in *Adarand* that federal affirmative action preferences would be subject to strict scrutiny just like state and local programs following *Wygant* and *Croson*. The circumstances that gave rise to the *Adarand* case began in 1989 when Mountain Gravel and Construction Company was awarded the prime contract for a federal highway construction project in Colorado. Federal law provided that Mountain Gravel would receive additional compensation if the company hired subcontractors certified as small businesses controlled by socially and economically disadvantaged individuals. The law also required a presumption that racial or ethnic minorities, including African Americans or Hispanics, were socially and economically disadvantaged. Mountain Gravel therefore had a financial incentive to award subcontracts to minority-owned businesses and thus awarded a subcontract for construction of the guardrail portion of the overall project to Gonzales Construction Company, despite the fact that another company, Adarand Constructors, a Colorado-based company that specialized in guardrail work, actually submitted the low bid for that portion of the project. Adarand, however, was not certified as a business controlled by socially and economically disadvantaged individuals. Representatives from Mountain Gravel indicated that they would have accepted Adarand's bid if they had not received additional payment for hiring Gonzales. Adarand filed suit in federal court, claiming that the race-based presumption used by the government in identifying socially and economically disadvantaged individuals violated the Fifth Amendment requirement that government not deny any person equal protection of the law. The District Court and Circuit Court of Appeals rejected Adarand's claims. The Supreme Court vacated the Circuit Court's opinion and remanded the case back to the lower courts for further proceedings.

In reaching its decision, the Supreme Court effectively repudiated the reasoning that had formed the basis for the earlier decisions in *Fullilove* and *Metro Broadcasting*. In those decisions, as noted earlier, the Court had argued that deference was due to Congress acting under legitimate constitutional authority and, therefore, that the less rigorous intermediate standard of equal protection review would be appropriate when considering challenges to racial preferences found in federal affirmative action programs. The Court reasoned in *Adarand*, however, that the equal protection requirements of the Fifth and Fourteenth Amendments were the same, and federal programs that included racial preferences should be subjected to strict judicial scrutiny just as state or local programs. In effect, this meant that federal affirmative action programs, like state or local programs, must serve a compelling government interest and must be narrowly tailored to meet that interest. The practical implication of this ruling was that federal affirmative action programs would have more difficulty withstanding constitutional scrutiny than they did previously.

Conflict in the Lower Courts

In the years since the 1995 *Adarand* decision, the Federal Circuit Courts of Appeals made a number of important rulings on affirmative action. One case from the Third Circuit addressed the statutory (Title VII) legality of affirmative action by a public employer. Several other cases, however, dealt explicitly with the constitutionality of affirmative action in the context of admissions policies for institutions of higher education. While some of the rulings in those cases were quite restrictive, others upheld affirmative action. This split on constitutional interpretation highlighted the need for a definitive ruling from the U.S. Supreme Court on affirmative action in university admissions. In each of these cases, strict scrutiny was applied, and the outcome turned on whether the Court considered student body diversity a sufficiently compelling interest for a state university to implement a preferential affirmative action program, and whether the programs under consideration were narrowly tailored. A review of the Third Circuit Title VII case will follow, as well as an analysis of the circumstances and outcomes of the cases involving constitutional interpretation.

Statutory Review

In 1996, in *Taxman v. Board of Education of Piscataway Township*, the Third Circuit Court of Appeals upheld a District Court repudiation of an affirmative action program implemented by a local school board.[2] The facts surrounding the case involved the consideration of race by the school board when it was forced to make a decision to lay off one of its teachers. In 1989, the Piscataway Board of Education faced the necessity of reducing by one the number of teachers it employed in its high school business department. The practice of the board was to require layoffs of teachers in reverse order of seniority. That is, those with less seniority were laid off prior to those with longer tenure. In this case, however, two teachers, Sharon Taxman and Debra Williams, who had been hired at the same time, were tied as the least senior business faculty members. Taxman and Williams were also considered equivalent in all other aspects of their qualifications. They taught similar classes and had received similar positive performance evaluations. In the past, when faced with such a situation, the board would have decided on a random basis who to retain and who to let go. In this instance, however, the board decided, consistent with its affirmative action plan, to keep Williams who was black and to lay off Taxman who was white. The board cited its desire to maintain some level of racial diversity among its faculty as a motivating factor for its decision. Williams was, in fact, the only African American teacher employed in the business department. In response, Taxman filed a charge of employment discrimination with the Equal Employment Opportunity Commission (EEOC). After attempts at conciliation were unsuccessful, the Department of Justice under the Bush administration filed suit against the board in the U.S. District Court for the district of New Jersey alleging a violation of Title VII, and Taxman intervened asserting her rights under Title VII. The District Court ruled in favor of Taxman.

The Board of Education appealed to the Third Circuit. The Circuit Court upheld the District Court decision arguing that the board's consideration of race did not fall within the parameters of legally permissible affirmative action set forth in the 1979 decision in the *United Steel Workers of America v. Weber*. Regarding that case, it should be remembered that the Supreme Court established that race might be considered in employment decisions so long as its consideration was to correct a manifest racial imbalance in the positions at issue. Affirmative action to maintain a specific balance, however, was not permitted under *Weber*, and thus the board's use of race to maintain racial diversity on its faculty was considered impermissible.

The board then appealed to the U.S. Supreme Court. The Court granted *certiorari*, but before oral arguments were heard, a coalition of civil rights groups, fearful that a conservative majority on the Supreme Court would use the case to further restrict affirmative action, came to the aid of the school board by assisting in the payment of a settlement of over $430,000 to Taxman and her attorneys. The case ended with the Third Circuit's decision intact.

Constitutional Review

From 1996 to 2001, five cases involving constitutional challenges to affirmative action in university admissions came before federal appeals courts for the Fifth, Sixth, Ninth, and Eleventh Circuits. The decisions across these courts were, as noted, fundamentally divergent, ultimately setting the stage for action by the Supreme Court. Because these cases focused on admissions policies of institutions of higher education, a key issue was whether diversity within a student body population was a sufficiently compelling state interest to allow affirmative action.

Hopwood v. State of Texas. The earliest of these decisions came in the case of *Hopwood v. State of Texas*.[3] At issue were admissions practices of the University of Texas School of Law, which was attempting to increase the enrollment of minority students through the use of an affirmative action program that contained racial and ethnic minority preferences. Under the program,

African American and Hispanic applicants were held to a lower standard for admission than were other applicants. This worked to the advantage of African Americans and Hispanics, but disadvantaged members of other minority groups and nonminorities. The plaintiffs, Cheryl Hopwood, Douglas Carvell, Kenneth Elliott, and David Rogers, were white applicants who were denied admission to the school. They challenged the law school's admissions program arguing that the use of minority preferences violated the equal protection clause of the Fourteenth Amendment.

The District Court upheld the program although it acknowledged that strict scrutiny was the appropriate standard of review. The Court found that the school's desire to achieve a diverse student body and to overcome the present effects of historic discrimination in the system of public education in Texas were compelling government interests and that the preferential admissions process was narrowly tailored to meet those interests. On appeal, the Fifth Circuit Court reversed and remanded the case arguing in part on the basis of precedents established in *Wygant* and *Croson* that student diversity and the goal of correcting the present effects of past discrimination by organizations other than the law school were not sufficiently compelling interests to permit the law school to utilize a system of racial and ethnic preferences in its admissions process. Thus, the affirmative action program was determined to be unconstitutional. In reaching its decision, the Court reasoned, in part, that "[t]he law school . . . presented no compelling justification, under the Fourteenth Amendment or Supreme Court precedent, that allows it to continue to elevate some races over others."[4] Following this decision by the Circuit Court, the state Attorney General issued an opinion prohibiting state institutions in Texas from developing preferential affirmative action programs. The law school appealed the Circuit Court decision to the U. S. Supreme Court, but because state law governing such programs had changed, the Supreme Court declined to hear the case arguing that the issues raised were rendered moot by the Attorney General's opinion. Thus, the Fifth Circuit's interpretation of the law was allowed to stand.[5]

Smith v. University of Washington School of Law. This case involved a challenge to the admissions policies of the University of Washington School of Law. During the 1990s, the law school used minority racial or ethnic status as a positive factor when considering individual applicants. The purpose of the policy was to help ensure the enrollment of a diverse student body. During this time, Katuria Smith and two other nonminority applicants who were denied admission to the law school brought suit on behalf of themselves and others similarly situated, claiming that the school's admissions policy violated Sections 1981 and 1983 of Title 42 of the United States Code and Title VI of the 1964 Civil Rights Act.[6] The District Court permitted the class action to proceed for injunctive and declaratory relief only. The injunction sought would have enjoined the law school from considering race in its admissions procedures, while the declaratory judgment sought would have been a statement from the court that the policy was in fact illegal.

Before the District Court was able to decide the case, the people of the state of Washington passed the ballot initiative (I-200), which, as was noted in chapter 3, prohibited the state from discriminating against or granting preferential treatment to any individual or group on the basis of race. Upon passage of I-200, the law school abandoned its consideration of race in admissions decisions. The District Court then denied Smith's request for injunctive and declaratory relief, noting that because I-200 prohibited the law school from engaging in the type of behavior that formed the basis for the initial claim, the issue was moot.

Of potentially greater significance, however, was the court's denial of a claim filed by Smith and the other plaintiffs for partial summary judgment. Smith and the others argued that summary judgment on their behalf was appropriate since, from their view, the Fourteenth Amendment prohibited any use of race as a factor in admissions procedures for the purpose of achieving student body diversity. The District Court denied Smith this claim relying on a reading of Justice Powell's opinion in *Regents of the University of California v. Bakke.*

The Ninth Circuit Court upheld the District Court on each of the aspects of its decision. With respect to the denial of summary judgment, the Circuit Court reasoned that Justice Powell's opinion in *Bakke* that student body diversity was a sufficiently compelling interest to permit a state university to use race as a factor in admissions decisions must be viewed as the opinion of the court. The Circuit Court concluded that it would "leave it to the Supreme Court to declare that the *Bakke* rationale regarding university admissions policies has become moribund, if it has."[7] The Ninth

Circuit would not make such a determination, arguing that until the Supreme Court revisits this issue, "it ineluctably follows that the Fourteenth Amendment permits University admissions programs which consider race for other than remedial purposes, and educational diversity is a compelling governmental interest that meets the demands of strict scrutiny of race-conscious measures."[8]

Johnson v. Board of Regents of the University of Georgia. In this case, the plaintiffs were three white women who were denied admission to the University of Georgia's fall 1999 class. The university's admissions policy provided for a preference for nonminority and male applicants in the form of a fixed numerical bonus added during the calculation of admission scores used to judge applicants. At issue in the case was whether the racial and gender preferences violated the equal protection clause of the Fourteenth Amendment of the U.S. Constitution. The district court found the preferences unlawful and entered a summary judgment in the plaintiffs' favor. The court argued that Justice Powell's opinion in *Bakke* was not binding precedent and that student body diversity did not constitute a compelling government interest necessary to justify the preferential policies in question. The university agreed to drop the consideration of gender in the admissions process but appealed the ruling with respect to the use of the racial preference.

The Eleventh Circuit affirmed the judgment of the District Court, but reached its conclusion without addressing the matter of whether Justice Powell's opinion in *Bakke* was binding precedent. The Circuit Court reasoned that even if student body diversity was found to be a compelling interest, the university's program would fail because it was not narrowly tailored. More specifically, the court found that the university used race in a "rigid or mechanical way that did not take sufficient account of the different contributions to diversity that individual candidates may offer" or of "race-neutral factors which may contribute to a diverse student body."[9] The Eleventh Circuit also found that the policy gave an "arbitrary . . . benefit to members of the favored racial groups," and that the school had not "genuinely considered, and rejected as inadequate, race neutral alternatives for creating student body diversity."[10] In announcing its opinion, the court argued that "[a] policy that mechanically awards an arbitrary 'diversity' bonus to each and every nonwhite applicant at a decisive stage in the admissions process, and severely limits the range of other factors relevant to diversity that may be considered at that stage, fails strict scrutiny and violates the Equal Protection Clause of the Fourteenth Amendment."[11] The university declined to appeal the ruling, stating that it would in the future focus on recruitment efforts to increase the enrollment of minority students.

Grutter and *Gratz*. Two additional cases involved challenges to admissions procedures at the University of Michigan, and ultimately, the outcomes of these cases have proved to be extremely important. One case, *Grutter v. Bollinger*, involved a Fourteenth Amendment challenge to law school admissions policies. The District Court for the Eastern District of Michigan found in this case that race was not "merely one factor which is considered among many others in the admissions process" but that the law school "places a very heavy emphasis on an applicant's race."[12] The trial court was persuaded that *Bakke* did not hold that a state educational institution's desire to assemble a racially diverse student body is a compelling governmental interest. The court stated that a distinction should be drawn between viewpoint diversity and racial diversity, arguing, "the educational benefits of the former are clear, those of the latter are less so."[13] The court also found that the defendants' use of race was not narrowly tailored and consequently ruled that the affirmative action plan was unconstitutional.[14]

The second case, *Gratz v. Bollinger*, involved a challenge to the University of Michigan undergraduate admissions procedures.[15] The plaintiffs here argued that the College of Literature, Science, and the Arts at Michigan had violated the equal protection clause of the Fourteenth Amendment by considering race as a factor in undergraduate admissions decisions. The District Court found that the school's admissions programs in existence at the time the case was filed in 1997 were unconstitutional, but that a later policy in effect for 1999 and 2000 was constitutional.[16]

Both Michigan cases were appealed to the Sixth Circuit Court of Appeals. With respect to *Grutter*, the Sixth Circuit overturned the District Court and ruled that the affirmative action admissions program was constitutional.[17] An appeal was made to the U.S. Supreme Court, which

decided to hear the case in order to clarify the issue of the constitutionality of affirmative action in public university admissions and resolve the
conflicts between the Fifth, Sixth, Ninth, and Eleventh Circuit Courts.
The Supreme Court also decided to consider the District Court opinion in
Gratz, although the Sixth Circuit had not yet ruled on that case.

The Supreme Court Steps In: The Michigan Cases and Affirmative Action in State University Admissions

As noted above, by the summer of 2002, two Circuit Courts of Appeals (the
Sixth and Ninth Circuits) had determined that preferential affirmative action in public university admissions was permitted under the Constitution,
while two other Courts of Appeals (the Fifth and Eleventh Circuits) had
found such policies failed to pass constitutional muster. The split between
the circuits was based in part on differing interpretations of Justice Powell's
opinion in *Bakke.* Guidance from the Supreme Court was needed to resolve
the dispute.

Grutter v. Bollinger at the Supreme Court

To better understand the issues raised in *Grutter,* some review of the
basic facts is necessary. To begin, we should note that Barbara Grutter was
a white, female resident of the state of Michigan who applied for admission
to the University of Michigan School of Law for the fall of 1996.[18] The Michigan Law School was highly selective in that it received annually more than
3,500 applications for approximately 350 seats in each entering class. Grutter had a 3.8 undergraduate grade point average and an admirable score
of 161 on the law school admissions test (LSAT). The law school initially
placed Grutter on a waiting list but subsequently denied her admission.
As noted earlier, she filed suit in federal district court (Eastern District of
Michigan), alleging that she was disadvantaged in the law school's admission process because of the school's use of an affirmative action plan. Grutter contended that the plan gave a limited preference to racial and ethnic
minorities in violation of the Fourteenth Amendment's guarantee of equal
protection of the law and statutory prohibitions on discrimination found
in Title VI of the Civil Rights Act of 1964 and Section 1981 of Title 42 of the

U.S. Code (derived from the Civil Rights Act of 1866). The District Court ruled in favor of Grutter, but, as previously discussed, that decision was reversed by the Sixth Circuit Court of Appeals.

The law school argued that its consideration of race was motivated by a desire to increase the diversity of its student body. Exposure to a diverse student body, the school argued, would better prepare students to function effectively in an increasingly diverse workforce and society. The presence of students with diverse values and backgrounds would "enhance classroom discussion and the educational experience" according to testimony offered before the District Court by a faculty member who chaired the committee that drafted the law school's policy.[19] Numerous *amicus* briefs were filed in support of the law school's position on the educational benefits of diversity among students.

Importantly, the law school's policy did not define diversity solely in terms of race or ethnicity. Rather, it was broadly defined to encompass all aspects of an applicant's social background. Part of the application process required the submission of a personal essay that would describe how an applicant would contribute to diversity. In addition, no fixed percentages or proportions were targeted for minority admissions. Race and ethnicity were to be considered as positive factors along with other facets of diversity, although the school was committed to the inclusion of students from groups such as African Americans, Hispanics, and Native Americans, who had historically suffered discrimination and would not likely be present in meaningful numbers without such a commitment.[20] In general, the policy required an assessment of "academic ability" along with a "flexible assessment" of individual "talents, experiences, and potential" for contributing to the general educational environment.[21] Admissions officials were required to evaluate each applicant based on all information in the file including the undergraduate grade point average, the LSAT score, letters of recommendation, a personal statement, and the essay describing how the applicant would contribute to diversity. Other variables, such as "the enthusiasm of recommenders, the quality of the undergraduate institution, the quality of the applicant's essay, and the areas and difficulty of undergraduate course selection" were also assessed.[22] The objective was to admit students who were diverse and academically outstanding.

The Supreme Court examined the law school's policy in the context of strict scrutiny. The first question considered was whether student body diversity was a sufficiently compelling state interest to permit preferential affirmative action designed to advantage racial or ethnic minorities. As we know, that issue was previously addressed in the *Bakke* case twenty-five years earlier. Of course, in *Bakke*, only Justice Powell applied strict scrutiny. Four justices held the affirmative action program at the medical school of the University of California at Davis to an intermediate standard of constitutional review and found it to be justified. Four others avoided the constitutional issue and voted to strike down the program on statutory grounds. Justice Powell provided a fifth vote for invalidating the medical school admissions program, but he also ruled that the Fourteenth Amendment did not prohibit the consideration of race in a properly constructed affirmative action plan.[23] Powell fashioned his view on the framework provided by strict scrutiny. He found diversity among students in state institutions of higher education to be a sufficiently compelling governmental interest to permit the consideration of race in admissions procedures, but as noted earlier, the Davis program was not, in his view, sufficiently narrowly tailored.[24]

The majority in *Grutter*, consisting of Justices O'Conner, Stevens, Souter, Ginsburg, and Breyer, reviewed Justice Powell's reasoning on student body diversity and weighed the considerable mass of *amicus* briefs outlining the ways in which diversity enriches student experiences. Justice O'Conner delivered the opinion of the Court, and noted that it has "long recognized that, given the important purpose of public education and the expansive freedoms of speech and thought associated with the university environment, universities occupy a special niche in our constitutional system."[25] The Court concurred with Justice Powell's opinion in *Bakke* that "the freedom of a university to make its own judgments as to education includes the selection of its student body."[26] In addition, the Court found the benefits of diversity within a university student body to be "substantial."[27] Those benefits included the promotion of interracial understanding, the erosion of racial stereotypes, and the development of students better prepared to enter a diverse society. Citing numerous studies entered into the record documenting the benefits of diversity, the majority endorsed Justice

Powell's view that student body diversity at state institutions of higher education was sufficiently compelling to justify the use of limited racial preferences in the admissions process. This was the first time that a majority of the Supreme Court had reached such an opinion.

The Court next turned to the question of whether the law school's consideration of race in its admissions process was narrowly tailored. The majority cited the individual review that each applicant's file received. It noted that the consideration of race was "flexible and nonmechanical."[28] No automatically determined set of bonus points was awarded for minority racial or ethnic status. Likewise, no quota or fixed number or proportion of seats in each entering class was reserved exclusively for minority applicants. Instead, the law school's goal of "attaining a critical mass of under-represented minority students" was sufficiently flexible to ensure that each applicant was reviewed as an individual, and all personal characteristics or aspects of an applicant's background beyond race and ethnicity, which could contribute to diversity, were given consideration.[29] For all of these reasons, the majority concluded that the race-conscious admissions program did not "unduly harm nonminority applicants."[30] The program was judged to be narrowly tailored, and it was upheld.[31] In short, the Court found that the constitutional guarantee of equal protection of the laws did not "prohibit the law school's narrowly tailored use of race in admissions decisions to further a compelling interest in obtaining the educational benefits that flow from a diverse student body."[32] Justice O'Conner noted the progress that had been made in the integration of higher education in the twenty-five years since Justice Powell's opinion in *Bakke*, and she stated at the conclusion of the majority opinion that "[w]e expect that 25 years from now the use of racial preferences will no longer be necessary to further the interest approved today."[33]

Gratz v. Bollinger at the Supreme Court

In this case, the reader will recall that an affirmative action program utilized in the undergraduate admissions policies of the College of Literature, Science, and the Arts at the University of Michigan was challenged. The suit was filed by two white applicants for admission: Jennifer Gratz, who had applied for the fall of 1995, and Patrick Hamacher, who had applied to enter during the fall of 1997. While both were found to be at least minimally qualified, ultimately, their applications were unsuccessful. They filed a class-action suit in October 1997 in the U.S. District Court for the Eastern District of Michigan.

Some knowledge of the nuances of the university's admissions procedures, which evolved considerably during the period in contention, is essential for an understanding of this case.[34] For the 1995 and 1996 freshman classes, the school calculated an index score known as the "GPA2" that combined an applicant's high school grade point average (GPA) with knowledge of other factors including the quality of the applicant's high school, the strength of the applicant's high school curriculum, any unusual circumstances endured by the applicant, the geographical location of the applicant's home, and whether the applicant was related to any university alumni. The GPA2 scores were then paired with American College Test (ACT) or Scholastic Aptitude Test (SAT) scores on two-dimensional tables with GPA2 scores arrayed vertically and ACT or SAT scores forming a horizontal axis. Cells within the tables would dictate whether students with corresponding scores would be admitted or rejected. The tables were constructed so that lower ACT or SAT scores were offset by higher GPA2 scores and vice versa. Importantly, however, in 1995 separate tables were constructed for in-state and out-of-state individuals from "underrepresented minority" groups including, according to the university, African Americans, Hispanics, and Native Americans, so that applicants from those groups could be admitted with GPA2 or ACT/SAT scores that were lower than those of other applicants. As a result, two applicants with identical GPA2 and ACT/SAT scores could be treated differently with respect to their admission to the university based upon their racial or ethnic status. Gratz was denied admission under this system.[35]

When considering applicants for the fall of 1997, the school changed its procedures so that the formula by which GPA2 scores were calculated explicitly included points for, among other things, under-represented minority status, socioeconomic disadvantage, or attendance at a high school with a predominantly underrepresented minority student body. It was under this system that Hamacher was refused admission.[36]

Admissions decisions made for the fall 1998 class were subject to a system modified still further. The university abandoned the use of admissions guidelines tables in favor of the establishment of a selection index.

Applicants received points on the index based on high school GPA, standardized test scores, the academic quality of their high schools, the rigor of their high school curriculum, in-state residency, relationships to alumni, the quality of their personal essays submitted with their applications, and their records of personal achievement or leadership. Additionally, under a "miscellaneous" category, applicants received twenty index points for being from an underrepresented minority racial or ethnic group (i.e., African American, Hispanic, and Native American). Index scores above 100 resulted in immediate admission, scores from 90 to 99 resulted in admission or a postponement, scores of 75 to 89 resulted in a delay of decision, and scores of 74 or below brought either a delay of decision or an immediate rejection. An Admissions Review Committee (ARC) was also established to provide additional consideration for applicant files "flagged" by admissions officers, who determined that the applicant had achieved a minimally acceptable selection index score and was determined to be worthy of further consideration based upon certain identified qualities or characteristics including underrepresented racial or ethnic status. In those cases, the ARC made the final admission decisions.

The District Court, following Justice Powell's opinion in *Bakke*, and based on the evidence presented, ruled that student body diversity was a sufficiently compelling interest to permit a preferential affirmative action plan as required under strict scrutiny analysis. The court also found the system used in 1999 and thereafter was narrowly tailored to meet that interest and, as a result, that program was determined to be constitutional.[37] The university's admission practices in place from 1995 to 1998, however, were not found to be narrowly tailored, and accordingly the court found those programs unconstitutional.

The case was appealed by both parties to the Sixth Circuit Court of Appeals. The Sixth Circuit heard the case on the same day it heard *Grutter*. As noted earlier, the Circuit Court delivered an opinion in *Grutter* upholding the University of Michigan Law School admissions program. The petitioners in *Grutter* appealed to the U.S. Supreme Court, which granted *certiorari* and also agreed to hear arguments in *Gratz* despite the fact that the Sixth Circuit had not yet ruled on the arguments offered by Gratz and Hamacher.

When considering *Gratz v. Bollinger*, the Supreme Court acknowledged that student body diversity was a compelling interest for a state university for the reasons it had set forth in *Grutter*. The Supreme Court disagreed with the District Court opinion in *Gratz*, however, by finding that the undergraduate admissions program used from 1999 on was not narrowly tailored and was therefore not permissible under the Constitution. The Court reasoned that the admissions system, which automatically awarded minority applicants twenty points on the selection index, did not provide the kind of individualized consideration of the applicants' contributions to diversity that Justice Powell had envisioned in *Bakke*. The automatic grant of twenty points, which amounted to one-fifth of what was needed for admission, made race the deciding factor for every minimally qualified, underrepresented minority applicant according to the Court. As a result, the part of the District Court opinion that had upheld the 1999 and 2000 undergraduate admissions system was overturned. Chief Justice Rehnquist delivered the opinion of the Court joined by Justices O'Connor, Scalia, Kennedy, and Thomas. Justice Breyer filed an opinion concurring in the judgment. Justices Stevens, Souter, and Ginsberg filed dissenting opinions.[38]

Implications of *Grutter* and *Gratz*?

In some respects, the significance of the *Grutter* and *Gratz* decisions is difficult to underestimate. The Supreme Court decisively settled the issue of whether diversity among students is a compelling interest for public universities and colleges. The Court decided that such diversity was indeed a compelling interest, and in the process, it swept away twenty-five years of ambiguity that had been the legacy of the *Bakke* decision. It is now clear that a properly constructed preferential affirmative action plan incorporated into higher education admissions processes is constitutionally acceptable. Furthermore, the specifics of the Michigan cases provide guidance as to how such a program might be properly constructed so that it is sufficiently narrowly tailored to meet the full requirements of strict scrutiny. Soon after the High Court's decisions in *Grutter* and *Gratz*, the University of Michigan issued a revised undergraduate admissions policy that includes short essays from applicants on the topic of diversity, which are reviewed to find students who will contribute to "the intellectual vibrancy and diversity of the student body."[39] The use of essays replaces the point system used in the previous affirmative action program, requires a significant number of additional application readers, and, as a result, costs as much as 33 percent more than the earlier system. However, the new process is designed to provide the individualized review that the Court found acceptable when preference is to be granted on the basis of race.[40] Preferential affirmative action to promote student body diversity in public universities now falls clearly within the constraints of the Constitution.

One may inquire, however, as to the implications of the Michigan decisions for preferential affirmative action in other contexts such as employment. Obviously, affirmative action in public employment may be challenged on constitutional equal protection grounds. Does the Court's finding preferential affirmative action constitutional in public college and university admissions systems mean that it will find preferential affirmative action acceptable in public employment? At first glance, the answer would appear to be that it does not. The implications of the Michigan decisions for public employment seem to be rather limited given that the focus in those cases was on student body diversity. A closer look, though, might suggest that such an interpretation is too restrictive and that broader implications for public employment may be present.

University admissions and employment are certainly distinct areas of concern. One might argue, for example, that the injury suffered by a qualified nonminority applicant denied admission to a highly selective college or university operating an affirmative action plan is less than that suffered by a similar person denied an employment opportunity because of affirmative action. The student whose application is turned down is likely to always have other choices for admission, although he or she may have to attend a less prestigious school; but the applicant seeking employment may frequently lack other options or alternatives, especially in times of economic distress and tight labor markets.[41] More broadly stated, "one who applies to a college or graduate school is a buyer, while one who applies for a job is a seller, and in general, those looking to spend money in exchange for a service have more options than those looking to sell their services in exchange for money."[42] Following this logic, if the limitation placed on nonminorities by affirmative action is greater in the employment context than in university admissions, the expectation might be that the Court would act more cautiously in that context.

To say conclusively that a nonpreferred job applicant *always* suffers greater harm than a nonpreferred college applicant is difficult, however. Individual circumstances vary so much that such a sweeping generalization cannot be sustained. But if the distinction in burden imposed on nonminorities by affirmative action in these two contexts is unclear, then perhaps less reason exists to limit the applicability of the principles articulated by the majority in the Michigan cases. Readers will recall that student body diversity was found to be a compelling interest largely because it was associated with the ability of colleges or universities to more effectively do their job of providing well-rounded educational experiences. That being the case, then, to the extent that persuasive arguments may be fashioned that diversity within the public workforce promotes effectiveness in the delivery of public services or operates to ensure that all interests are represented in the decision-making processes of public agencies, such diversity might well be considered a compelling governmental interest. In specific contexts, a positive relationship between workforce diversity and effective service delivery has been documented. For example, minority representation among the employees of certain social service agencies whose clients consist disproportionately of minority citizens will help to ensure better service delivery for those citizens.[43] Similarly, the presence of minority police officers at work in predominantly minority neighborhoods is often beneficial.[44] In addition, as reviewed in chapter 4 of this work, studies have found that work force diversity and productivity can be complementary concepts.[45] The growing literature on representative bureaucracy also discussed in chapter 4 is certainly relevant here. As was noted, that literature indicates that in a number of contexts the presence of minority employees in a public agency helps to ensure that minority interests will not be overlooked as policy decisions are being fashioned.[46] One might argue then, at least in some contexts, that public workforce diversity may alone provide a sufficiently compelling interest to support preferential affirmative action because it helps to ensure that agencies can more effectively accomplish their missions. When affirmative action programs are narrowly devised to meet that interest, they could be constitutionally permissible.

Indeed, the Seventh Circuit Court of Appeals has already made such a determination in the context of the Chicago police department. In *Petit v. Chicago*, decided December 15, 2003, the Seventh Circuit ruled that police force diversity is a compelling government interest based on evidence of a positive correlation between racial and ethnic diversity in the workforce and effectiveness of the agency.[47] The court found also that the means the city used to achieve diversity, which involved fashioning a promotional examination specifically for minority officers by taking into account that some questions on the usual examination were biased in favor of nonminority officers, was found to be narrowly tailored. The court reasoned that the alteration was necessary to eliminate the advantage provided by the unaltered test to nonminority officers. The U.S. Supreme Court refused to hear an appeal of the Seventh Circuit decision in June of 2004, but the question of whether the type of reasoning applied by the Court of Appeals will ultimately prevail in the Supreme Court remains unanswered.[48]

Any finding that preferential affirmative action is constitutionally permissible does not mean, however, that a government organization must implement such a policy. It simply means that government has the opportunity to do so if it chooses. Government may choose not to engage in affirmative action, and prohibitions on affirmative action may be incorporated into public law as was done in California and the state of Washington. Ward Connerly, who led the successful effort to ban preferential affirmative action in those states, along with Jennifer Gratz, launched a signature drive to place a state constitutional amendment prohibiting preferential programs before Michigan voters in November 2004. That effort was dealt a setback, however, in late March of 2004, when a state circuit court judge ruled that the wording on the petitions being circulated did not fully inform voters of the effect of the initiative and was, therefore, in violation of the law governing the state's constitutional amendment process. The state was ordered to rescind its approval of the petitions.[49] Signatures were finally submitted in January of 2005 in an attempt to place the initiative on the November 2006 ballot. The Michigan Board of State Canvassers refused to certify the measure, however, in July of 2005 citing evidence of misrepresentation by those who circulated the petitions. The Michigan Civil Rights Initiative, the organization formed by Connerly and Gratz to push the amendment, took the issue back to Court, and on December 20,

2005, a Michigan Court of Appeals ruled that the initiative will be on the November 2006 ballot.[50]

In Summary: Where Do We Stand at the Beginning of a New Century?

Where are we in 2005 with regard to the legality of preferential affirmative action programs? After nearly three decades of litigation, some points are clear. Statutory constraints on such programs, which provide the only legal limitations on private organizations, are not excessively restrictive. As long as a preferential program is targeted to address a manifest racial or gender imbalance in traditionally segregated job categories, does not trammel the rights of nonminorities or men, and is constructed as a temporary strategy, it will survive statutory review under Title VII. Specific guidelines for such programs are articulated in the *United Steelworkers of American v. Weber* and *Johnson v. Transportation Agency* decisions.[51] Constitutional limitations, which apply only to government programs, however, impose a much tighter boundary on affirmative action. Since the mid-1980s, and the outcome of the *Wygant* case, state and local government programs were in effect required to survive strict judicial scrutiny when challenged on constitutional grounds. The *Croson* decision of 1989 reinforced that requirement, and the *Adarand* decision of 1995 extended that standard to federal government programs. Strict scrutiny requires that the distinctions embedded in a preferential affirmative action plan serve a compelling government interest and be narrowly tailored to meet that interest. The need to correct the present effects of past discrimination by an employer was judged to provide a compelling interest, but numerous other justifications for affirmative action have been struck down. The University of Michigan cases of 2003 provided judicial recognition of student body diversity as a new justification for preferential affirmative action, in the context of public university admissions policies. The future implications of the Michigan cases for affirmative action in public employment are, as we have seen, uncertain.

This state of development of the law leaves us in a rather interesting position. Because statutory constraints are less restrictive in practice than those grounded in the constitution, private organizations are granted greater latitude in fashioning preferential affirmative action programs than are government organizations. One might argue, however, that government has an obligation at least as great as that of the private sector to deal effectively with the problem of discrimination that has disadvantaged minorities and women. Perhaps the government obligation is even higher given the importance of government action as a symbol or example for private organizations to follow. If the government cannot effectively combat historic patterns of discrimination, how can it be expected to effectively regulate the private sector? Whether the duality of standards of legal permissibility for the public and private sectors will endure is not clear. As always, much will depend on the future composition of the Supreme Court. The retirement of Justice O'Connor and the death of Chief Justice Rehnquist in late 2005 led to two new appointments. Judge John G. Roberts, who was confirmed as the new Chief Justice on September 29, 2005, and Judge Samuel A. Alito, Jr., confirmed on January 31, 2006, to fill the remaining open seat, have both expressed views in opposition to affirmative action early in their careers. The Roberts appointment, and that of Alito, could be decisive. Evidence of the actual impact of affirmative action on minorities and nonminorities, which is the topic of discussion in the next chapter, will also, no doubt, be important in future deliberations.

seven

Evidence on the Effectiveness of Affirmative Action

We now turn to a consideration of the impacts of affirmative action on employment and educational opportunities for minorities and women. The question of impact is obviously important. Arguments arrayed in favor of the policy are seriously undermined if it cannot be demonstrated that affirmative action is effective in assisting members of targeted groups. Indeed, evidence that affirmative action is ineffective would substantially strengthen the position of those opposed to the policy whose arguments have been outlined in preceding chapters. As a result, much depends on the empirical evidence that speaks to the impact of affirmative action. Arguments made by proponents and opponents of the policy are inherently testable. Discussions of affirmative action should be informed by such research.

As we embark on a brief review of the relevant research literature, however, readers should bear in mind two contextual issues. First, determining if a policy of interest is effectively reaching its goals might initially appear to be a relatively simple matter. This proposition would seem especially true when the goals themselves are not obscure or unsettled, and certainly, a general clarity about the goals of affirmative action is present—the policy is intended to benefit women and minorities in employment and other contexts. Yet to conclude that affirmative action or any other policy is effective, analysts must first be able to accurately estimate what the condition at issue would have looked like in the absence of the policy and must establish with relative certainty that any positive changes observed in that condition are in fact the result of the policy rather than the outcome of other events or processes. These interrelated concerns are linked directly to the nature of the research design utilized to assess impact. The quality of the underlying design, that is, its ability to rule out extraneous influences, will determine the extent to which the results can be trusted.[1] In the context of affirmative action in employment, for example, it is important that its effects be distinguished from those of non-discrimination policy more generally, as well as from the effects of litigation brought by minorities or women to combat discrimination or other factors that could impact employment trends. The studies reviewed here rely on research designs that provide reasonably strong bases for assessing impact.

A second issue that should be considered is that regardless of affirmative action's instrumental effects on minorities and women, a symbolic aspect of the policy exists, which to many proponents would alone provide adequate justification for the policy's continuation. In other words, affirmative action is a symbol of an organization's commitment to addressing the problems of women and minorities caused by discrimination.[2] It is a clear indication that such discrimination is unacceptable and must be overcome. In this way, affirmative action signals hope for groups that suffer the despair of discrimination, and proponents argue that the creation of hope in those circumstances can only accrue to our benefit.

Affirmative Action in Employment

Despite the growth of preferential affirmative action programs since the 1970s, only a relatively small number of scholars have been interested in assessing the impact of those efforts on employment opportunities for minorities and women. While the debate over affirmative action emerged almost immediately, the argument was often conducted in the absence of good evidence of the policy's effectiveness. Nevertheless, several rigorous studies have been conducted. The earliest of those focused largely on the effects of affirmative action programs for government contractors. One study, for example, examined data from over 74,000 private firms in 1970 and 1972 in order to determine whether the economic position, measured by employment and wage shares of minorities or women, improved more in firms with federal government contracts as opposed to those without such contracts.[3] Contractors were, of course, required to comply with federal affirmative action guidelines. The findings indicated that black men who worked for contractor firms benefited significantly more than those in noncontractor firms. The benefit for black men was even greater in those firms that had been subjected to Office of Federal Contract Compliance Programs (OFCCP) compliance reviews. Thus, it appeared that affirmative action was useful in improving the economic circumstances of black men. A similar effect for black women, however, could not be demonstrated. The authors found no significant differences in employment or wage shares for black women in contractor and noncontractor firms.[4]

Another important work, which examined businesses subjected to OFCCP compliance reviews in the late 1970s, found even more positive effects of affirmative action goals and timetables. Jonathan S. Leonard found that goals established for minority and female employment had a significant positive impact on employment shares of members of those groups.[5] The firms that established goals to increase the employment of minorities and women experienced substantial growth in the representation of members of those groups in their workforces. As a result, Leonard concluded that the policy had been largely effective. The author found similar results in two additional studies published in 1984.[6]

A study by Johnson and Welch published in 1976, however, raised questions about the effectiveness of affirmative action.[7] These authors investigated the potential impact of affirmative action on the distribution of labor income. They found that a rigidly enforced affirmative action policy would result in a significant portion of skilled nonminority workers not being fully utilized and that minority workers experienced income gains relative to majority workers. While the policy's proponents would suggest that these were expected outcomes, the authors of this study argued that these results would, in turn, lower the incentives for minority workers to accumulate higher skill levels while raising that incentive for majority workers, thereby ultimately exacerbating problems of income inequality.

Similarly, Griffin, writing in 1992, also reported potentially negative implications of affirmative action.[8] This work tested the proposition that because affirmative action constrains a firm's hiring practices, a firm implementing affirmative action will experience less elastic demand for inputs and higher output costs than a firm not so constrained. Griffin found that for firms subject to affirmative action requirements in 1980, costs rose by an average of 6.5 percent relative to unconstrained firms. In other words, while affirmative may have been effective in increasing employment shares for minority workers, higher costs were associated with doing so.

Another study, this one from 2000, demonstrated that affirmative action had differential effects on different targeted groups. In an examination of unemployment rates from 1961 to 1983, Bisping and Fain found that nonwhite men lost ground relative to nonwhite and white women.[9] Their results suggest that in response to affirmative action pressure, firms first hired white women and then nonwhite women. As a consequence, the duration of unemployment for nonwhite (black) men increased. The authors caution that numerous social changes during the period under analysis make it impossible to decisively link the trends they observed to the implementation of affirmative action, but they argue that their findings are consistent with the incentive structures provided to discriminatory employers under affirmative action.

Research published in the fall of 1992, however, focusing simply on employment, stressed the positive impact of affirmative action programs by 131 private firms in the Detroit, Michigan, metropolitan area in 1972.[10] The authors interviewed senior managers, personnel administrators, and first line supervisors to collect data on their employment practices. Their findings indicated that firms with affirmative action programs in place were more likely than other firms to hire black men into management positions. In addition, firms with affirmative action received more applications from women for management positions but were not more likely to hire women. Also, firms that had already employed larger shares of women and black men received more applications from members of those groups. The authors suggested that this underscored the importance of informal channels of communication operating through an existing workforce regarding the availability of job opportunities and the attractiveness of particular firms as employers. As a result, affirmative action efforts that are successful in bringing minorities and women into a firm initially may have the added benefit of creating momentum for the further employment of members of those groups.

A more recent study, published in 2002 and focused on the construction industry, also found that affirmative action had a large positive impact on the employment of women.[11] Data were collected from construction firms involved in highway projects in Boston, Los Angeles, and Oakland in the 1980s and 1990s. Similarly, another recent study from 2003, examining data from 167 randomly selected firms in six cities in Florida also found positive impacts of affirmative action.[12] Employers who supported affirmative action employed proportionately larger shares of blacks at all levels, but particularly in higher-level jobs.

Other newer studies, nevertheless, have been less optimistic. For example, in 1999 Becker, Lauf, and Lowery examined employment rates for women and minorities in the journalism and mass communications industry looking for evidence that affirmative action has had an impact.[13] From comparative time-series analyses, they found that women had made gains in recent years relative to men, but that the situation for minorities relative to nonminorities had actually deteriorated. Their findings suggest that while affirmative action may have been effective in helping women in this industry, it had apparently not been beneficial for minority group members since their employment levels had declined relative to those of nonminorities.

Additional research has examined the impact of affirmative action on minority and female employment in the public sector. Some work, for example, has focused on the impact of numerical goals and timetables in the federal civil service.[14] As we know, goals and timetables, which imply the potential use of racial or gender preferences, were first authorized by the U.S. Civil Service Commission for use by federal agencies in May of 1971. An examination of time-series data on federal employment (government-wide) of blacks from 1962 through 1984 and women from 1967 through 1984 revealed mixed results. In general, no evidence suggested a positive impact of preferential affirmative action on employment of blacks. For example, modest increases in the employment of blacks in middle and higher-level federal pay grades, areas where black underrepresentation was highest, continued in the years following the authorization of the use of goals and timetables at almost exactly the same rate as before the policy change. In the highest grades examined (General Schedule [GS] and equivalent grades 12–18), the proportion of the workforce comprised of blacks was increasing at a rate of 0.22 percentage points per year on average before the policy change. That is, the black share of federal employment in those grades was increasing at a rate of slightly less than one-fourth of one percentage point per year during that time. In the period following the decision to permit agencies to use affirmative action goals and timetables, the employment of blacks rose at a rate of 0.27 percent per year. The rate had increased only an imperceptible 0.05 percent or five one-hundredths of one percent per year. Thus, the addition of numerical goals and timetables to federal affirmative action policy, which had earlier been based primarily on recruitment and training efforts alone, had little apparent effect on the employment of blacks in these grades when data from all agencies were aggregated.

Evidence on the employment of women was quite different, however. In both the middle (GS 7–12) and higher-level (GS 13–18) grades examined, the policy of permitting goals and timetables in federal agency affirmative action plans was followed by significant increases in the rate of gain in female employment. For example, in the middle grades, women had increased their employment share by 0.54 percent per year prior to goals and timetables, but that rate increased to an average gain of 1.25 percent per year from 1972 to 1984. For the higher grades, the change was from a 0.10 percent increase per year (one-tenth of one percent) to a rate of 0.62 percent per year following the shift in the policy. These changes in female employment trends are consistent with a positive impact of affirmative action. But did the policy change produce observed increases in the rate of gain in the employment of women? Was the accelerated entry of women into the workforce more generally, which began in earnest in the early 1970s, a factor? It is impossible to tell with certainty. Time-series research designs cannot separate the effects of a given policy change or intervention from those of other historic events that occur at or about the same time, and with that in mind, the evidence for effectiveness of goals and timetables on the employment of women should be viewed cautiously.

Before rushing to the conclusion that goals and timetables were not effective, however, readers should recall that the 1971 policy transformation only authorized federal agencies to utilize that approach to affirmative action; it did not require them to do so. As a result, perhaps many or several of the largest agencies did not develop preferential affirmative action programs, at least in the 1970s, and the absence of the actual use of that approach may account for the lack of evidence of impact as in the case of black employment. While the full extent of the utilization or lack of utilization of goals and timetables by federal agencies in the period examined remains unknown, an examination of individual agency employment trends revealed wide variation in the extent to which black and female employment rates increased. Additionally, a detailed examination of the implementation of equal employment opportunity and affirmative action programs in two agencies, one that significantly increased the rate of growth in black and female employment following the 1971 authorization of goals and timetables and another that did not do so, revealed that the agency with the better record of increases in black and female employment made extensive use of goals and timetables, while the agency with the poorer record established no goals for minority or female employment. This finding suggests a positive impact of affirmative action, but additional research would be useful to reinforce that conclusion.

The work of economists Harry Holzer and David Neumark has been useful in that regard. In studies published in 1999 and 2000, these scholars found that firms using affirmative action had higher levels of employment of minorities and women than nonaffirmative action firms. Largely consistent with earlier findings by Leonard, businesses with affirmative action employed about 15 to 20 percent fewer white men than firms without affirmative action programs. Holzer and Neumark also found, however, that minority employees in establishments with affirmative action tended to be less well qualified than nonminority workers in terms of readily observable measures of qualifications such as levels of formal education, but that affirmative action firms recruited much more extensively and used more intensive job screening mechanisms, which suggests that they may have uncovered other information about minority workers that offset the lower levels of education. The authors found little evidence that minority workers hired under affirmative action performed more poorly than nonminority workers. With regard to women employed by firms with affirmative action programs, there was no significant difference between their qualifications and those of men in the same racial groups and no evidence of weaker performance. The data analyzed by Holzer and Neuman were from representative surveys of approximately 3,000 employers in four large urban areas: Atlanta, Boston, Detroit, and Los Angeles. Affirmative action hiring was practiced by employers covering about 42 percent of the work-force in the samples studied.[15]

Holzer and Neumark also conducted exhaustive reviews of the empiri-cal literature on the effects of affirmative action in 2000 and 2005. The au-thors reviewed studies examining the impact of affirmative action on em-ployment and educational opportunity for minorities and women, as well as research on the share of government contracts held by firms owned by minorities and women. While the studies examined used different meth-odologies and data sources, there was substantial consistency in results, which led Holzer and Neumark to conclude that overall there was "com-pelling evidence that affirmative action does increase employment, enroll-ments [in institutions of higher education], and contracting for minori-ties and women in the ways we might expect."[16] In addition, the authors found from their reviews that affirmative action in employment had no significant negative effect on productivity or performance in organizations where it was practiced.

In summary, then, the work by Holzer and Neuman suggests that affir-mative action does have redistributive effects in favor of groups (racial and ethnic minorities and women) who have suffered discrimination histori-cally, although the effects are not huge. Opportunities for white men de-cline under affirmative action, but only modestly. There is little evidence of weaker performance by the beneficiaries of affirmative action.[17]

Affirmative Action in Higher Education

Employment and career progress for minorities and women, as for all in-dividuals, is ultimately linked to educational opportunities. Higher edu-cation, in particular, provides an avenue through which people may pass into many of the most lucrative and rewarding careers. An opportunity to obtain a college or university degree, therefore, can be fundamentally important in shaping life outcomes. In the early 1970s, as preferential affir-mative action in employment and government contracting began, admis-sions programs at many colleges and universities were modified to include special minority recruitment efforts and goals for minority enrollment.[18]

As we have seen, these programs almost immediately sparked controversy and litigation, and by the mid-1990s a number of courts were restricting preferential policies. The states of California and Washington prohibited such programs by state constitutional referendum. Much of the debate over affirmative action in college and university admissions has taken place without consideration of empirical evidence on the effects of those programs on minority populations. Yet some evidence is available, and perhaps the most extensive review to date is that undertaken by William G. Bowen and Derek Bok published in 1998.

Bowen and Bok, former presidents of Princeton and Harvard Universities, respectively, suggest that the flow of students from secondary schools into colleges and universities and on to work and careers is analogous to that of a river.[19] The course of the river has twists and turns. It runs deep in places and shallow in others. The flow of the river is the product of a range of policy decisions, but before informed decisions can be made, according to Bowen and Bok, the "shape of the river" must be known.[20]

To develop that understanding, Bowen and Bok collected data from 80,000 students who matriculated in 1951, 1976, and 1989 at twenty-eight academically selective institutions of higher education that have "strict limits on the number of places in an entering class and far more qualified applicants than places."[21] Under those conditions, the authors assert, admissions decisions become most difficult and ethnic or race-based preferences may be most critical.[22] Data from twenty-four private and four public universities are included in their analysis.

Findings regarding the impact of affirmative action at those schools are striking. First, black enrollment and graduation were found to have increased remarkably following the initiation of preferential affirmative action in the 1970s.[23] That trend helped lead, in turn, to a dramatic growth in the number of blacks in professional and administrative occupations and the emergence of a more visible black middle class. Moreover, there was no question that black students admitted under affirmative action policies were qualified to occupy the seats they held. They competed effectively with their white counterparts and graduated at comparable rates.[24] Black students generally reported no stigma or demoralization associated with affirmative action admissions, and black and white students reported positive experiences from interaction between the races.[25]

Bowen and Bok also estimate the likely impact of a termination of preferential affirmative action policies and a move to race-neutral admissions procedures on black and white students. They find that such an approach would dramatically reduce the probability of a black applicant being admitted but, as was briefly noted in chapter 1, would only marginally increase the probability of admission of a white student. More specifically, the authors found that the overall probability of admission for black applicants would fall from 42 percent (actually observed in 1989 in five schools examined) to an estimated value of 13 percent.[26] Within those same schools, the white probability of admission would rise by only 1.5 percentage points from 25 percent to 26.5 percent by shifting to a race-neutral policy. The estimated impact of ending preferential affirmative action on the actual enrollment of black students is even more striking. Based on an analysis of data from the same five selective schools, the prediction was that black enrollment would fall from 7.1 percent to between 2.1 and 3.6 percent, depending on what assumptions are made regarding the rate at which admitted blacks actually enroll.

Data from the University of California at Berkeley immediately following the termination of preferential affirmative action on that campus further illustrates this pattern. At Berkeley, the black probability of admission fell from 48.5 percent in 1997 to 15.6 percent in 1998, while the white probability of admission rose from 29.9 percent to 30.3 percent.[27] This resulted in a decline in black enrollment from 6.8 percent to 2.4 percent. The termination of affirmative action, thus, had a dramatic negative impact on black students, but because blacks and other targeted minorities comprised such a small proportion of student enrollment at Berkeley compared to whites even when affirmative action was in place, the termination of affirmative action did not lead to a significant increase in white student admissions.

Bowen and Bok point to the presence of parking spaces reserved for the disabled as a useful analogy for affirmative action preferences.[28] They attribute the analogy to Thomas Kane who argues that "eliminating the reserved space would have only a minuscule effect on parking options for non-disabled drivers. But the sight of the open space will frustrate many passing motorists who are looking for a space. Many are likely to believe that they would now be parked if the space were not reserved."[29] The proportion of all spaces that is reserved for disabled drivers is extremely small, however, and if the spaces were not reserved, at any given time a passing driver would likely find them occupied.

A closer look at data from the entire University of California system following termination of preferential affirmative action provides additional insight. Recall that the Regents voted to prohibit schools from considering race and ethnicity in the admissions process in 1995, and Proposition 209 passed in the fall of 1996. These events resulted in an immediate decline in the number of applications from members of underrepresented minority groups. This suggested that even though the ban on consideration of race and ethnicity was not implemented until the application and admissions cycle for the fall 1998 entering class was under way, many minority students apparently were choosing not to apply as early as 1996. This decline may have occurred because minority students saw California schools as not particularly hospitable places since they knew their probability of admission had declined. The system-wide decline in applications from under-represented minority students was accompanied by a similar decline in admissions and enrollment. As a result, only 15.5 percent of the 1998 freshman class was drawn from underrepresented groups, although those groups comprised close to 40 percent of the state's population.[30] By comparison, in 1995 students from these groups comprised 21 percent of incoming freshmen system-wide. Since 1998, underrepresented minority enrollment has rebounded a bit. For example, 19 percent of the fall 2002 freshman class consisted of students from underrepresented minority groups. But to achieve that result, the system has redoubled its outreach and recruitment efforts and has significantly expanded its interaction with high schools serving large numbers of Hispanic and African American students.

While the system-wide rebound is laudable, data from that level obscure the full story.[31] As has been stressed earlier, affirmative action was significant in the state's most selective schools, especially Berkeley and UCLA. As previously noted, there was a decline in the admission of black students to Berkeley following the implementation of the ban on preferential affirmative action in 1998 and an accompanying decline in black enrollment. Similar declines were experienced by Native Americans and Hispanics. In fact, the number of students from underrepresented minority groups admitted fell from 1,778 (25.3 percent of all admits) for the fall of 1997 to 717 (11.0 percent of all admits) for the fall of 1998, a drop of 1,061 such students.

A similar decline was recorded at UCLA, where underrepresented minority admits fell from 2,010 (21.2 percent of all admits) for the fall of 1997 to 1,282 (13.5 percent of the total) for the fall of 1998. By the fall of 2003, students from underrepresented groups comprised 17.3 percent of all admissions at Berkeley and 16.9 percent at UCLA, but those numbers were still far below the 1997 numbers. The system-wide rebound noted earlier was the result of substantial growth in the admission of underrepresented minority students at the *less selective* schools in the system, especially the University of California, Riverside, where total admission of all students increased dramatically and that of students from underrepresented minority groups grew from 20.6 percent for the fall of 1997 to 26.9 percent for the 2003 freshman class.[32] In terms of raw numbers, that increase represents a change from 1,488 students from underrepresented groups in 1997 to 4,055 in 2003. Thus, the termination of preferential affirmative action in California has had a significant and enduring negative impact on minority enrollment at the state's most selective campuses.

Conclusion

Given the magnitude of the controversy over preferential affirmative action, fewer systematic efforts have been undertaken to determine the impact of the policy than one might expect. The debate and literature on affirmative action have largely been concerned with arguments over the desirability of the policy and the extent to which it provides a just solution for the problems of minorities or women caused by discrimination without an explicit examination of its impact. This situation is unfortunate, since whether the policy provides a solution at all will depend in large part on whether it is effective in promoting opportunities for members of targeted groups. If affirmative action is ineffective, it becomes much more difficult to defend. Indeed, even if affirmative action has a positive impact on minorities and women, the potential costs to organizations implementing it and to nonminority men should be considered as well.

The research evidence reviewed here is representative of the existing empirical literature on affirmative action. In general, it shows that preferential affirmative action can be beneficial for minorities and women in a number of settings. Studies that have examined the policy in the context

of private-sector contractors have shown dramatically positive results. Preliminary evidence from the federal civil service also shows that goals and timetables have made a difference. Some work has shown that the policy has a differential impact on women and minorities, however, and nonminority men do bear some cost to the extent that they have fewer opportunities than they would have had otherwise.

Evidence in the context of college and university admissions is also generally positive. Data collected by Bowen and Bok build a strong case for the constructive impact of affirmative action on minority students, and the experience in California's colleges and universities following the termination of preferential affirmative action in admissions procedures further illustrates the impact of the policy. When affirmative action was ended, minority admission and enrollment fell dramatically at the state's most selective schools. At the same time, the probability of admission for white applicants increased only by the smallest of margins. The implications in this context are that affirmative action has worked to benefit minorities considerably. The cost of the program in terms of lost opportunities for white students is quite limited.

Additional research, in both employment and educational settings, would, of course, be useful. Such work should be designed carefully to assess the impact of the policy in terms of benefits for minorities and women and potential costs for others. The differential impact affirmative action may have on different targeted groups should also be explored further. Do women benefit more than minority men? How has the growth of the Hispanic population in the United States affected the availability of opportunities for African Americans or other minorities? What has been the effect of affirmative action on Asian Americans? Questions could also be raised about the usefulness of our traditional racial and ethnic categories and whether they should be reconsidered. Where do people of mixed race or ethnic origin fit into this picture? The relationship between affirmative action and diversity management programs deserves further attention as well. If diversity management is operationally different from traditional affirmative action, does it have the same kind of impact? These are only a few of the questions to be addressed in future research.

eight

Affirmative Action in the Twenty-first Century

Affirmative action has been at the center of the struggle over discrimination for nearly forty years. As we have seen, it has generated substantial controversy. An abundance of positive and negative views on the subject is available, but often those opinions are formed without a full understanding of the history of affirmative action, its various forms, and the legal framework within which it operates. Hopefully, this book will help to promote a greater understanding of those issues, although disagreement over the policy will likely endure as long as affirmative action continues.

The dispute over affirmative action exists largely because the policy seeks to influence the distribution of jobs, seats in colleges and universities, and other valued opportunities. The distribution of advantage that affirmative action is designed to alter, however, is one that has, in part, rested upon long-enduring patterns of discrimination that have been directed against racial and ethnic minorities and women. Affirmative action developed as a means of combating such discrimination and its effects. It consists of a variety of programs intended to assist minorities and women in job markets, admission to institutions of higher education, and other settings. Affirmative action involves efforts to reach out to members of groups that have historically suffered discrimination to encourage them to apply for jobs or other opportunities and in some instances to ensure that they receive training. Since the late 1960s and early 1970s, the policy has included the establishment of numerical goals and limited preferences for minority and female selection.

The earlier approaches to affirmative action, which focused on recruitment and training, were controversial when they began in earnest in the early 1960s, but they are much less contentious in the twenty-first century. In fact, those practices, which rest squarely on the principle of nondiscrimination, are rarely the subject of discussion today.

The development of goals for selection of minorities or women or other related forms of preference is the focus of controversy and has eclipsed recruitment and outreach efforts in the public perception of affirmative action. Opponents of preferences have argued that such programs violate notions of nondiscrimination and have suggested that former policies of racial or gender neutrality are more just. Readers should bear in mind, however, that preferential affirmative action has not, as a practical matter, moved this country from behaviors grounded on neutrality to policies favoring minorities and women. The preferences involved are, in large part, a compensatory mechanism designed to remediate the effects of past discrimination. They are also designed to move us more rapidly than a policy of strict nondiscrimination would allow to a state of affairs in which our national diversity is reasonably well reflected across all levels of our institutions.

Preferential affirmative action does not mean that people should receive jobs or other opportunities for which they are unqualified. Such practices are not permitted under legally constructed affirmative action programs. Undoubtedly, less-qualified individuals have benefited under affirmative action. However, as noted earlier, precise gradations in levels of qualifications are usually difficult to determine, and any selection process is subject to abuse. Proponents argue that when properly implemented, preferential affirmative action will involve the establishment of goals or other strategies favoring the selection of qualified minorities or women for positions in which they are significantly underrepresented based on a reasonable estimation of what equitable representation would look like. Affirmative action goals must be tied, in other words, to fair estimates of the availability of minorities and women with requisite knowledge, skills, and abilities for the positions sought. Many consider such a policy a justifiable and well-reasoned means of dealing with discrimination, which has limited the options available to women and people of color, even if the policy does not always lead to the selection of the very best or most highly qualified person. Opponents find such an outcome unsatisfactory.

Much of the argument over affirmative action has not been about its effectiveness. As we have seen, much of the empirical evidence indicates that affirmative action increases opportunities for minorities and women. Indeed, it is likely that the effectiveness of the policy has helped to make the dispute more contentious. When effective, affirmative action policy imposes costs on groups, primarily white males, who may have had greater opportunities were it not for affirmative action. It also imposes administrative costs on organizations that must establish procedures to implement the policy. Ironically, the policy's apparent effectiveness has also led some opponents to argue that so much progress has now been made in the struggle against discrimination that affirmative action is no longer necessary. Those who adhere to this view argue that discrimination against minorities and women is no longer a significant problem. The advocates for affirmative action are quick to point to evidence, however, showing that is not the case.

Some of the most persuasive evidence of continuing problems of discrimination is found in studies that have sent matched pairs of minority and nonminority job applicants with equal credentials to inquire about job openings. Under those conditions, white applicants routinely receive more interviews and job offers than do African Americans or Hispanics. Studies by the Urban Institute in the 1990s, for example, utilized pairs of job seekers in Chicago and Washington, D.C., to inquire about job openings advertised in newspapers.[1] The pairs of applicants were assigned identical qualifications for the positions except that in each case one applicant was white and one was either African American or Hispanic. In 20 to 36 percent of the inquiries the minority applicant was either denied an opportunity for employment (e.g., told the job was filled) while the white applicant was not, or the minority applicant was subjected to long delays, was offered an inferior position, or was offered inferior wages or benefits.[2] Other studies with similar results were conducted and published in 1994 and 1996.[3]

This research supplements a long line of analyses in economics documenting wage gaps between individuals of different races, ethnicities, and sexes that remain unexplained after the effects of a variety of human capital and productivity variables have been controlled statistically. The residual gap in wages between racial, ethnic, and sex groups uncovered in such studies is viewed as evidence of discrimination.[4] These outcomes suggest that while much of the most open and blatant discrimination against racial and ethnic minorities may have ended, subtle and less visible discriminatory actions persist.

One conclusion that can be reached from research documenting the enduring presence of discrimination against racial and ethnic minorities in labor markets is that policies designed to combat such behavior should not be abandoned. Preferential affirmative action is one of those policies. Opponents to those approaches argue, however, that alternative efforts grounded on nondiscrimination, which give no preference on the basis of race, ethnicity, or sex, are more consistent with American values and better serve principles of justice. An end to this debate is not likely as long as preferential affirmative action continues to operate.

Before closing this discussion about affirmative action, a final summary of the ways in which it originates may be useful. First, affirmative action may be implemented because it is mandated by a court order. The Civil Rights Act of 1964, Title VII, gives federal courts the authority to order affirmative action as a remedy when they find that an employer has been in violation of the law. This is the only way in which affirmative action is truly forced upon an employer. All other instances in which affirmative action occurs—including times when an employer enters into a consent agreement calling for affirmative action as a way of settling a discrimination law suit filed by minorities or women—are the result of employers voluntarily agreeing to implement the policy. Programs established by the federal government or state or local governments within their own civil service systems are also established voluntarily. The same is true of programs established by public universities or colleges. Likewise, programs established by the federal government or state or local government, which require private businesses with whom they enter into contractual agreements for the provision of goods or services to implement affirmative action programs, are voluntary in the sense that the government is not compelled to establish such programs, and the businesses are not compelled to seek government contracts. All other affirmative action programs that exist in the private sector also result from voluntary efforts. In other words, government has voluntarily (without the pressure of litigation) established affirmative action programs within the public workforce, in public colleges and universities with respect to student admissions, and as a condition placed upon firms with whom government enters into contracts. In addition, whether affirmative action is voluntary or nonvoluntary, it may take the form of recruitment and outreach efforts, goals and timetables, or other preferential strategies.

The Supreme Court has ruled that under specified circumstances, reviewed earlier in chapter 5 of this work, preferential affirmative action programs do not violate the law as set forth in Title VII. This ruling means that private sector firms and businesses may implement preferential affirmative action programs provided they comport with the guidelines set by the Court. The Supreme Court has also found that preferential affirmative action programs are permissible under the Constitution, although the rationale for those programs and the constraints which limit them are much more narrowly construed, and the focus of recent cases has been limited to admissions programs for institutions of higher education.

The future of affirmative action hinges on two points. The Supreme Court could change its mind and rule that preferential programs are no longer acceptable under any conditions, under either Title VII or the Constitution. This scenario seems unlikely, however, given the Court's most recent decisions about affirmative action, and given the fact that the Court has never come close to making such a ruling throughout its long history of dealing with the issue. Nevertheless, recent changes in the composition of the Court could result in changes in rulings on affirmative action. Alternatively, legislatures could write laws, or constitutional amendments could be enacted prohibiting all forms of preferential affirmative action. This kind of action would be most likely in the presence of a broad-based political consensus in opposition to preferential programs. Even though opponents were successful in securing state constitutional prohibitions in California and the state of Washington, such a consensus is doubtful nationally, given the continuing problem of discrimination.

In sum, at this point, we have thoroughly examined the development of affirmative action policy in the United States. The forms that affirmative action policy may take and the varied implications of those differing approaches for values such as nondiscrimination have been reviewed. The legal status of affirmative action has been discussed, and the progress that has been made in the struggle to assist groups that have historically suffered discrimination because of race, ethnicity, and sex has been noted. We know that much of that progress can be attributed to the operation of affirmative action programs. We have also witnessed the controversy over affirmative action, especially the conflict associated with preferential forms of the policy.

The 2003 decision by the Supreme Court in *Grutter v. Bolliner* buoyed supporters of affirmative action policy and established its legal foundation in the context of university admissions. Although the Court has found affirmative action policy to be legally permissible under specific circumstances, its ruling does not guarantee that governmental or other organizations will continue to find affirmative action desirable. Nevertheless, affirmative action will be endorsed by a number of observers for some time to come, and certainly, justification for it may be found so long as problems of discrimination persist. Support for affirmative action is unlikely to end completely until sufficient progress has been made in the battle against discrimination—and minorities and women are no longer disadvantaged in their efforts to achieve employment or educational opportunities because of race, ethnicity, or sex. The truth is that American society has not yet reached that point. Although advances have been made, much is still left to be done. When minorities or women are represented in positions below expected levels, given their representation among those with requisite qualifications, proponents will argue that affirmative action designed to benefit members of those groups is warranted. Affirmative action programs properly constructed can be an effective means of helping to ensure that society will enjoy the benefits of the great diversity this nation offers.

Notes

Notes to Chapter One

1. For early discussion of the controversy over affirmative action, see U.S. Senate, Committee on the Judiciary, Subcommittee on Separation of Powers, *Hearings: The Philadelphia Plan and S. 931*, 91st Congress, 1st Session, October 27–28, 1969. For examples of later analyses that give insight into the unfolding of the affirmative action debate, see Charles H. Levine, "Beyond the Sound and Fury of Quotas and Targets," *Public Administration Review*, vol. 34, no. 3 (May/June, 1974), pp. 240–41; Thomas Sowell, "Affirmative Action Reconsidered," *The Public Interest*, no. 42 (winter 1976), pp. 47–65; and William Raspberry, "Fill in the Numbers Please," *Washington Post*, July 15, 1983, p. A23.

2. In the mid-1990s, as the debate escalated, the popular press contained numerous articles on the pros and cons of affirmative action. For a sampling of that literature, see B. Drummond Ayres Jr., "Conservatives Forge New Strategy to Challenge Affirmative Action," New York Times, February 16, 1995, p. A1; Mary Frances Berry, "The Case for Affirmative Action," *Emerge*, vol. 6, no. 7 (May 1995), pp. 28–37, 40–43, 48; John F. Harris and Kevin Merida, "Affirmative Action under Fire: The Public Consensus That Supported Federal Efforts Has Been Imperiled," *Washington Post National Weekly Edition*, vol. 12, no. 25 (April 24–30, 1995), pp. 6–7; Jeffrey Rosen, "Affirmative Action: A Solution," *The New Republic*, vol. 212, no. 19 (May 8, 1995), pp. 20–25; Robert L. Woodson, Sr., "Affirmative Action Has Accomplished Little for Most Blacks," *Emerge*, vol. 6, no. 7 (May 1995), pp. 42–43; and James Traub, "The End of Affirmative Action (And the Beginning of Something Better)," *New York Times Magazine* (May 2, 1999), pp. 44–51.

3. The California and Washington state initiatives are reviewed in greater detail in chap. 3. A general discussion of California's Proposition 209 is also contained in J. Edward Kellough, Sally Coleman Selden, and Jerome S. Legge Jr., "Affirmative Action under Fire: The Current Controversy and the Potential for State Policy Retrenchment," *Re-*

view of Public Personnel Administration, vol. 17, no. 4 (fall, 1997), pp. 52–74. Perhaps the most thorough treatment of Proposition 209, however, is found in the book by Lydia Chavez titled *The Color Bind: California's Battle to End Affirmative Action* (Berkeley: University of California Press, 1998). Voters in Houston, Texas, rejected a similar proposal in November 1997 that would have prohibited preferential affirmative action by that city. It is interesting to note, however, that the Houston initiative spoke of ending "affirmative action," while the California and Washington state initiatives spoke of ending "discrimination" and "preferential treatment."

4. See Executive Order 99281, November 9, 1999, Executive Office of the Governor, State of Florida, accessed December 30, 2005 through the government section of the official Florida state Web site at www.myflorida.com.

5. In 1997, for example, anti-affirmative action legislation was introduced in Congress and in fifteen different state legislatures. See chap. 3 of this book for further discussion. See also Kellough, Selden, and Legge, "Affirmative Action under Fire."

6. One such law firm, known as the Center for Individual Rights (CIR), is located in Washington, D.C. The CIR has played a part in several important cases. For an early discussion of this organization, see Terry Carter, "On a Roll(back)," *ABA Journal,* vol. 84, no. 2 (February 1998), pp. 54–58.

7. *Adarand Constructors v. Pena, U.S. Secretary of Transportation*, 515 U.S. 200 (1995).

8. *Hopwood v. State of Texas,* 78 F. 3d 932 (1996).

9. *Texas et al. v. Hopwood et al.*, 518 U.S. 1033 (1996). See also Norma M. Riccucci, "The Legal Status of Affirmative Action: Past Developments, Future Prospects," *Review of Public Personnel Administration*, vol. 17, no. 4 (fall 1997), pp. 22–37. The CIR (supra, note 6) played an important role in opposition to affirmative action in the *Hopwood* case.

10. This is certainly the argument made by Stephan and Abigail Thernstrom in a provocative book on race relations in America. The Thernstroms document substantial progress made by African Americans since the 1930s and argue that in the current context most affirmative action programs are not necessary or justified. See Stephan Thernstrom and Abigail Thernstrom, *America in Black and White: One Nation Indivisible* (New York: Simon and Schuster, 1997).

11. See Barbara R. Bergmann, "Is Discrimination a Thing of the Past?" in

In Defense of Affirmative Action (New York: Basic Books, 1996), chap. 2, for a discussion of this problem. See also, U.S. Merit Systems Protection Board, *A Question of Equity: Women and the Glass Ceiling in Federal Employment* (Washington DC: Government Printing Office, October 1992). Discussion of the continuing problem of discrimination is also found in George Stephanopoulos and Christopher F. Edley Jr., *Affirmative Action Review: Report to the President* (Washington DC: Government Printing Office, 1995); Christopher F. Edley, *Not All Black and White: Affirmative Action, Race, and American Values* (New York: Hill and Wang, 1996); and, more recently, in Justice Ginsburg's dissent in *Gratz v. Bollinger*, 539 U.S. 244 (2003). Ginsburg cites numerous additional sources documenting the continuing problems of inequality and discrimination faced by racial and ethnic minorities in America. This issue is also discussed briefly in chap. 8 below.

12. Harold D. Lasswell, *Politics: Who Gets What, When, and How* (New York: Smith, 1936).

13. United States, *Federal Register*, March 8, 1961, pp. 1977–79 (Washington, DC: Government Printing Office, 1961).

14. United States, *Federal Register*, September 28, 1965, pp. 12319–25 (Washington, DC: Government Printing Office, 1965). The Kennedy and Johnson executive orders are discussed further in chap. 2.

15. David H. Rosenbloom makes the point, however, that with respect to the equal employment opportunity program for the federal civil service, the U.S. Civil Service Commission (CSC) moved to authorize goals and timetables for other reasons. Primarily, people at the CSC were concerned that if they did not develop a more aggressive approach, Congress would shift authority for federal equal employment opportunity to the U.S. Equal Employment Opportunity Commission. See David H. Rosenbloom, "The Civil Service Commission's Decision to Authorize the Use of Goals and Timetables in the Federal Equal Employment Opportunity Program," *Western Political Quarterly*, vol. 26, no. 2 (June 1973), pp. 236–51.

16. Nathan Glazer, *Affirmative Discrimination* (Cambridge, MA: Harvard University Press, 1987), pp. x–xi.

17. On this issue, see *United States v. Paradise*, 480 U.S. 149 (1987), esp. the discussion on p. 189.

18. Civil Rights Act of 1991 (105 Stat. 1971).

19. "Bush Cites 'Quotas' in Rights Bill Veto," *Congressional Quarterly Almanac* (Washington, DC: Congressional Quarterly Inc., 1990), p. 472.

20. James E. Jones Jr. "The Genesis and Present Status of Affirmative Action in Employment: Economic, Legal, and Political Realities," *Iowa Law Review*, vol. 70 (1985) pp. 901–44.

21. Other traits or circumstances include, among other things, the presence of a disability or status as a military veteran. Sections 501 and 503 of the Rehabilitation Act of 1973 (87 Stat. 355) provide for affirmative action by the federal civil service and by government contractors, respectively, for disabled persons, although preferential forms of affirmative action are not authorized. The Vietnam Era Veterans' Readjustment Assistance Act of 1974 (88 Stat. 1578) provides for similar affirmative action by government contractors to assist Vietnam era veterans.

22. Of course, some policies redistribute resources from the "have-nots" to the "haves." Regressive tax policies, which are quite common, are an excellent example.

23. For a discussion of affirmative action as redistributive policy, see Edley, *Not All Black and White: Affirmative Action, Race, and American Values.* See also, Louis M. Guenin, "Affirmative Action in Higher Education as Redistribution," *Public Affairs Quarterly*, vol. 11, no. 2 (April 1997), pp. 117–40.

24. This is true in the case of affirmative action targeted toward racial or ethnic minorities because, first, members of those groups comprise by definition a minority of the general population, and second, minorities with the requisite qualifications for selection into positions where they are currently underrepresented typically constitute less that the total minority population. As a result, the inclusion of qualified minorities in competition for various opportunities will not significantly diminish the odds of selection of any nonminority individual. William G. Bowen and Derek Bok in *The Shape of the River: Long-Term Consequences of Considering Race in College and University Admissions* (Princeton, NJ: Princeton University Press, 1998) demonstrate this fact clearly with respect to preferential affirmative action in the admissions programs at highly selective colleges and universities. The argument is perhaps more difficult to make with regard to affirmative action targeting women and the detrimental effect that policy has on the odds favoring selection of any given male applicant. It would still hold, however, in cases where women are currently underrepresented and the inclusion of previously excluded qualified women did not substantially increase the overall size of the selection pool. For example, if an applicant pool expanded

from fifty individuals to sixty following the inclusion of women, the odds of any particular man being selected decline only from 0.020 to 0.016. For further discussion of this point, see chap. 7 below.

25. See *Regents of the University of California v. Bakke*, 438 U.S. 265 (1978). See also, Howard Ball, *The Bakke Case: Race, Education, and Affirmative Action* (Lawrence: University Press of Kansas, 2000).

26. Thernstrom and Thernstrom, *America in Black and White*, p. 431.

27. See *United Steel Workers of America v. Weber*, 443 U.S. 193 (1979) and *Johnson v. Transportation Agency, Santa Clara, California*, 480 U.S. 616 (1987).

28. The Fourteenth Amendment applies to the states and explicitly prohibits the denial of equal protection of the laws. The Fifth Amendment, which applies to the federal government, contains a due process clause that has been interpreted to prohibit the denial of equal protection of the laws. See *Bolling v. Sharpe*, 347 U.S. 497 (1954).

29. See *Firefighters v. Stotts*, 467 U.S. 561 (1984) and *Wygant v. Jackson Board of Education*, 476 U.S. 267 (1986).

30. See *Fullilove v. Klutznick*, 488 U.S. 488 (1980); *City of Richmond v. J.A. Croson Company*, 488 U.S. 469 (1989); and *Metro Broadcasting v. Federal Communications Commission*, 497 U.S. 547 (1990).

31. *Adarand Constructors v. Pena, U.S. Secretary of Transportation*, 515 U.S. 200 (1995).

32. *Grutter v. Bollinger et al.*, 539 U.S. (2003).

33. *CBS Evening News*, Transcript, January 18, 1998, p. 7; available from Burrelle's Transcripts, P.O. Box 7, Livingston, NJ 07039-0007.

34. CBS Evening News, p. 7.

35. *Adarand Constructors v. Pena, U.S. Secretary of Transportation*, Part III-D, 515 U.S. 235–37 (1995).

36. *Regents of the University of California v. Bakke*, 438 U.S. 265 (1978). See the opinion of Justice Powell, Part V-C at p. 320, in which Justices Blackmun, Brennan, Marshall, and White concurred.

37. *Wygant v. Jackson Board of Education*, 476 U.S. 267 (1986) and *City of Richmond v. J.A. Croson Company*, 488 U.S. 469 (1989).

38. *Grutter v. Bollinger et al.*, 539 U.S. 306 (2003).

39. On this theoretical perspective, see Kathleen Thelen and Sven Steinmo, "Historical Institutionalism in Comparative Politics," in *Structuring Politics: Historical Institutionalism in Comparative Analysis*, ed. Sven Steinmo, Kathleen Thelen, and Frank Longstreth (New York: Cambridge University Press, 1992), pp. 1–32. See also, James G. March and John P. Olsen, "The New Institutionalism: Organizational Factors in Political

Life," *American Political Science Review*, vol. 78, no. 3 (September 1984), pp. 734–49.

Notes to Chapter Two

1. Unfortunately, many such ironies can be found. The Constitution, with its three-fifths clause, initially sanctioned the institution of slavery, and in many other ways the founding incorporated inequality. Women could not vote until well into the twentieth century. For decades before that, property ownership was required for white men to be eligible to vote. A classic argument, which was first developed by Charles Beard in 1913 in his book titled *An Economic Interpretation of the Constitution of the United States*, is that the founders framed the Constitution as they did primarily to protect economic interests, rather than to promote equality.

2. Gunnar Myrdal, *An American Dilemma: The Negro Problem and Modern Democracy* (New York: Harper and Row, 1944).

3. The Thirteenth, Fourteenth, and Fifteenth Amendments to the Constitution passed after the Civil War abolished slavery, established citizenship for former slaves, prohibited states from denying persons due process or equal protection of the laws, and guaranteed all citizens the right to vote. In addition, the Civil Rights Acts of 1866, 1870, 1871, and 1875 were designed to help secure these and other civil rights. Nevertheless, discrimination and violence against blacks and other minority groups were largely unabated in much of the country, and no administrative program was established to effectively deal with that problem under the post–Civil War statutes. The Bureau of Refugees, Freedmen, and Abandoned Lands, otherwise known as the Freedmen's Bureau, was established by Congress in 1865 and operated until 1872, but it focused its activities on providing food, health care, and education to former slaves. The Bureau did not confront the problem of discrimination directly but instead concentrated on the provision of aid, through such actions as the establishment of black schools and medical facilities.

4. United States, *Statutes at Large*, vol. 53, part 2, August 2, 1939, pp. 1147–48 (Washington, DC: Government Printing Office, 1939).

5. United States, *Statutes at Large*, vol. 54, part 1 (November 26, 1940), p. 1214 (Washington, DC: Government Printing Office, 1940).

6. United States, *Federal Register*, November 13, 1940, pp. 4445–48 (Washington, DC: Government Printing Office).

7. For a thorough discussion of Randolph and the proposed 1941 march on Washington, see Herbert Garfinkel, *When Negroes March: The March on Washington Movement and the Organizational Politics of the FEPC* (Glencoe, IL: Free Press, 1959). See also, Merl E. Reed, *Seedtime for the Modern Civil Rights Movement: The President's Committee on Fair Employment Practice 1941–1946* (Baton Rouge: Louisiana State University Press, 1991). Other works with excellent treatments of these developments include Samuel Krislov, *The Negro in Federal Employment: The Quest for Equal Opportunity* (Minneapolis: University of Minnesota Press, 1967); and David H. Rosenbloom, *Federal Equal Employment Opportunity: Politics and Public Personnel Administration* (New York: Praeger, 1977).

8. Krislov, *The Negro in Federal Employment*, p. 30.

9. Krislov, *The Negro in Federal Employment*, p. 30, and Reed, *Seedtime for the Modern Civil Rights Movement*, pp. 13–14.

10. Krislov, *The Negro in Federal Employment*, p. 30.

11. United States, *Federal Register*, June 27, 1941, p. 3109 (Washington, DC: Government Printing Office, 1941).

12. Reed, *Seedtime for the Modern Civil Rights Movement*, p. 15. Reed's assertion does not consider work by the federal government's Bureau of Indian Affairs to assist in the assimilation of Native Americans in the late nineteenth and early twentieth centuries.

13. Reed, *Seedtime for the Modern Civil Rights Movement*, p. 15.

14. Reed, *Seedtime for the Modern Civil Rights Movement*, p. 156. See also, Ruth P. Morgan, *The President and Civil Rights: Policy-Making by Executive Order* (New York: St. Martin's Press, 1970), p. 31.

15. Reed, *Seedtime for the Modern Civil Rights Movement*, p. 46.

16. Governor Dixon's comments are cited in Reed, *Seedtime for the Modern Civil Rights Movement*, p. 91.

17. Reed, *Seedtime for the Modern Civil Rights Movement*, pp. 91 and 115.

18. United States, *Federal Register*, May 29, 1943, pp. 7183–83 (Washington, DC: Government Printing Office, 1943).

19. Reed, *Seedtime for the Modern Civil Rights Movement*, p. 112.

20. Reed, *Seedtime for the Modern Civil Rights Movement*, pp. 156–57; Morgan, *The President and Civil Rights*, p. 31.

21. Reed, *Seedtime for the Modern Civil Rights Movement*, pp. 158–61.

22. Reed, *Seedtime for the Modern Civil Rights Movement*, pp. 321–38.

23. Rosenbloom, *Federal Equal Employment Opportunity*, p. 63.

24. Morgan, *The President and Civil Rights*, pp. 40–41.

25. United States, *Federal Register*, July 28, 1948, pp. 4311–13 (Washington,

DC: Government Printing Office). In addition, an accompanying order, Executive Order 9981, required that the armed services be deseg-
regated. For a full discussion of that issue, see Morgan, "Equality in the
Armed Services," in *The President and Civil Rights*, chap. 2, pp. 10–27.

26. Morgan, *The President and Civil Rights*, p. 53. The FEB made this very point
in its *First Report* issued on September 30, 1949. See Morgan, chap.3, p.
93, note number 63.

27. Rosenbloom, *Federal Equal Employment Opportunity*, p. 64.

28. United States, *Federal Register*, December 6, 1951, p. 12303 (Washington,
DC: Government Printing Office).

29. The fair employment practices committees established subsequently
by the Eisenhower and Kennedy administrations were also funded in
this manner. See Morgan, *The President and Civil Rights*, p. 31.

30. Morgan, *The President and Civil Rights*, pp. 42–43.

31. Morgan, *The President and Civil Rights*, p. 54.

32. Morgan, *The President and Civil Rights*, p. 44. Executive Order 10479 can be
found in United States, *Federal Register*, August 13, 1953, p. 4899.

33. Morgan, *The President and Civil Rights*, p. 54.

34. United States, *Federal Register*, January 19, 1955, pp. 409–11.

35. United States, *Federal Register*, March 8, 1961, pp. 1977–79.

36. Kennedy's Committee, like those of Eisenhower, was an interdepartmental committee. See, *supra,* note 29.

37. Rosenbloom, *Federal Equal Employment Opportunity*, p 67. Rosenbloom
quotes passages from the President's Committee on Government Employment Policy, *Fourth Report* (Washington, DC: Government Printing
Office, 1961), p. 12.

38. United States, *Federal Register*, March 8, 1961, p. 1977.

39. United States, *Federal Register*, March 8, 1961, p. 1977.

40. Morgan, *The President and Civil Rights*, p. 47.

41. For a review of data collected during the Kennedy years, see U.S. Civil
Service Commission, *Study of Minority Group Employment in the Federal Government* (Washington, DC: Government Printing Office, 1965).

42. Civil Service Commission, *Study of Minority Group Employment in the Federal
Government*.

43. Rosenbloom, *Federal Equal Employment Opportunity*, p. 8.

44. Christopher Pyle and Richard Morgan, "Johnson's Civil Rights Shake-
up," *The New Leader*, vol. 48, no. 20 (October 11, 1965), pp. 3–6.

45. Pyle and Morgan, "Johnson's Civil Rights Shake-up," p. 4.

46. Pyle and Morgan, "Johnson's Civil Rights Shake-up," p. 4.

47. United States, *Federal Register*, September 28, 1965, pp. 12319–25 (Washington, DC: Government Printing Office, 1965).

48. Pyle and Morgan, "Johnson's Civil Rights Shake-up," p. 5.

49. See Edward J. McVeigh, "Equal Job Opportunity within the Federal Government: Some Experiences of the Department of Labor in Establishing Positive Measures to Assure Full Compliance with Civil Rights and Executive Orders," *Employment Security Review*, vol. 5, nos. 7 and 8 (July/August 1968), pp. 42–47.

50. United States, *Federal Register*, October 17, 1967, pp. 14303–4 (Washington, DC: Government Printing Office, 1967).

51. See, for example, U.S. Civil Service Commission, *Study of Employment of Women in the Federal Government* (Washington, DC: Government Printing Office, 1967).

52. Coverage of Title VII of the Civil Rights Act of 1964 was finally extended to the federal civil service and to state and local government employment as a result of amendments accomplished through the Equal Employment Opportunity Act of 1972. See United States, *Statutes at Large*, vol. 86, part 1, March 24, 1972, p. 103 (Washington, DC: Government Printing Office, 1972).

Notes to Chapter Three

1. For an excellent discussion of the OFCCP, see Hugh Davis Graham, *The Civil Rights Era: Origins and Development of National Policy, 1960–1972* (New York: Oxford University Press, 1990), pp. 282–90.

2. Graham, *The Civil Rights Era,* p. 281.

3. Graham, *The Civil Rights Era,* p. 287.

4. For a detailed discussion of this problem, see R.W. Fleming, "The Building Trades and Title VII of LMRDA," in *Symposium on LMRDA: The Labor-Management Reporting and Disclosure Act of 1959*, ed. Ralph Slovenko (Baton Rouge, LA: Claitor's Bookstore Publishers, 1961), pp. 1033–48. The Taft-Hartley Act can be found at United States, *Statutes at Large*, Vol. 61, Part 1, 1947, pp. 1361–62.

5. United States, *Statutes at Large*, Vol. 73, 1959, p. 545.

6. Graham, *The Civil Rights Era,* p. 289.

7. Graham, *The Civil Rights Era,* pp. 291–97.

8. J. E. Jones Jr., "The Origins of Affirmative Action," *University of California, Davis Law Review,* vol. 21 (1988), pp. 383–419.

9. Graham, *The Civil Rights Era,* p. 325.

10. Graham, *The Civil Rights Era,* p. 325.

11. Graham, *The Civil Rights Era,* p. 340.

12. *Contractors Association of Eastern Pennsylvania v. Secretary of Labor,* 311 F. Supp. 1002 (1970). The decision was affirmed by the Third Circuit Court of Appeals and the Supreme Court denied *certiorari,* thus allowing the District and Circuit Court decisions to stand.

13. United States, Department of Labor, Revised Order No. 4, Vol. 41, CFR Part 60-2 (1970).

14. On this point, see David H. Rosenbloom, *Federal Equal Employment Opportunity: Politics and Public Personnel Administration* (New York: Praeger, 1977), pp. 102–5.

· 15. J. E. Jones Jr. "The Genesis and Present State of Affirmative Action in Employment: Economic, Legal, and Political Realities," *Iowa Law Review,* vol. 70 (1985), pp. 901–44.

16. United States, *Statutes at Large,* Vol. 86, Part 1, March 24, 1972, p. 103.

17. U.S. Congress, House of Representatives, Committee on Government Operations, *Reorganization Plan No. 1 of 1978: Message from the President of the United States,* 95th Congress, Second Session, House Document No. 95-295.

18. See J. Edward Kellough and David H. Rosenbloom, "Representative Bureaucracy and the EEOC: Did Civil Service Reform Make a Difference?" in Patricia W. Ingraham and David H. Rosenbloom, eds., *The Promise and Paradox of Civil Service Reform* (Pittsburgh: University of Pittsburgh Press, 1992), pp. 245–66.

19. U.S. Equal Employment Opportunity Commission, Management Directive 714, October 6, 1987.

20. U.S. Commission on Civil Rights, *For All The People . . . By All the People: A Report on Equal Opportunity in State and Local Government Employment* (Washington, DC: Government Printing Office, 1969).

21. Commission on Civil Rights, *Report on Equal Opportunity,* pp. 91–92.

22. Commission on Civil Rights, *Report on Equal Opportunity,* p. 108.

23. *Griggs et al., v. Duke Power Company,* 401 U.S. 425 (1971).

24. See *Teamsters v. United States,* 431 U.S. 324 (1977).

25. See *Uniform Guidelines on Employee Selection Procedures,* 29 CFR, Section 1607. For an examination of the impact of the *Uniform Guidelines* in municipal hiring practices, see Christopher Daniel, "Selection's Uniform Guidelines: Help, Hindrance, or Irrelevancy?" *Review of Public Personnel Administration,* vol. 9, no. 2 (Spring 1989), pp. 68–78.

26. *Ward's Cove Packing Company v. Atonio,* 490 U. S. 642 (1989).

27. *Ward's Cove Packing Company v. Atonio*, p. 660.

28. *Ward's Cove Packing Company v. Atonio*, p. 670

29. *Ward's Cove Packing Company v. Atonio*, pp. 678–79.

30. "Bush Cites 'Quotas' in Rights Bill Veto," *Congressional Quarterly Almanac* (Washington, DC: Congressional Quarterly Inc., 1990), p. 472.

31. United States, *Statutes at Large*, Vol. 105, Part 2, pp. 1071–1100.

32. *Seminole Tribe v. Florida*, 517 U.S. 44 (1996).

33. States can be sued, however, by any private party whose constitutional rights they have allegedly violated.

34. *Alden et al. v. Maine*, 527 US 706 (1999).

35. See *Seminole Tribe v. Florida*, 517 U.S. 44 (1996) and *Fitzpatrick v. Bitzer*, 427 U.S. 445 (1976).

36. *Kimel v. Florida Board of Regents*, 528 U.S. 62 (2000).

37. *Kimel v. Florida Board of Regents*.

38. *Board of Trustees of the University of Alabama v. Garrett*, 531 U.S. 356 (2001). For a discussion of the implications of this case, see Christine L. Kuykendall and Stefanie A. Lindquist, "*Board of Trustees of the University of Alabama v. Garrett*: Implications for Public Personnel Management," *Review of Public Personnel Administration*, vol. 21, no. 1 (Spring 2001), pp. 65–69.

39. S. A. Holmes, "Programs Based on Sex and Race Are under Attack: Dole Seeks Elimination," *New York Times*, March 16, 1995, p. A1.

40. George Stephanopoulos and Christopher Edley Jr., *Affirmative Action Review: Report to the President* (Washington, DC: Government Printing Office, 1995).

41. Drummond B. Ayres Jr., "Conservatives Forge New Strategy to Challenge Affirmative Action," *New York Times*, February 16, 1995, p. A1.

42. In an interview with the Bureau of National Affairs, James Joy, executive director of the American Civil Liberties Union of Colorado, indicated that citizen groups were collecting signatures for a 1998 ballot proposal to ban affirmative action programs (Bureau of National Affairs, 1997). However, no anti–affirmative action initiatives were placed on the ballot in 1998.

43. In Washington, two initiative options are available. The first is to gather the requisite signatures and have the measure placed on the ballot. The second is to obtain the needed signatures and present the initiative to the legislature. The legislature then has three options: (a) pass the initiative as written, which does not have to be approved by the governor; (b) do nothing and the initiative is placed on the next

ballot; and (c) alter the initiative and both versions are placed on the next ballot.

44. J. Edward Kellough, Sally Coleman Selden, and Jerome S. Legge Jr., "Affirmative Action under Fire: The Current Controversy and the Potential for State Policy Retrenchment," *Review of Public Personnel Administration*, vol. 17, no. 4 (fall 1997), pp. 52–74. The present discussion of anti–affirmative action efforts in the states draws heavily from this source.

45. See Kellough, Selden, and Legge, "Affirmative Action under Fire." See also a study by the Leadership Conference on Civil Rights Education Fund/Americans for a Fair Chance, Anti-Affirmative Action Threats in the States: 1997–2004 (June 2005), available at www.fairchance.org, accessed December 29, 2005.

46. Kellough, Selden, and Legge, "Affirmative Action under Fire," pp. 66–69.

47. Guy Coates, "Foster Takes Aim at Affirmative Action," *Houston Chronicle*, January 12, 1997, p. A9.

48. Executive Order 99-281, November 9, 1999, Executive Office of the Governor, State of Florida. The order stated in Section 1 that "neither the Office of the Governor nor any Executive Agency may utilize racial or gender set-asides, preferences or quotas when making decisions regarding the hiring, retention or promotion of a state employee." An equivalent prohibition on set-asides, preferences, or quotas was also announced in Section 2 with respect to the making of state contracting decisions. Section 3 of the order requested that "the Board of Regents implement a policy prohibiting the use of racial or gender set-asides, preferences or quotas in admissions to all Florida institutions of Higher Education, effective immediately."

49. The remarks were delivered by Governor Jeb Bush on November 9, 1999, at the time of the issuance of his executive order ending preferential affirmative action. A copy of the remarks was found online at www.flgov.com in January 2000.

50. Remarks by Bush on November 9, 1999.

51. On this point, see DeWayne Wickman, "Jeb Bush's Good (Not Perfect) Affirmative Action Alternative," *USA Today*, November 30, 1999, p. A19. An additional viewpoint is provided by Clarence Page, "Affirmative Action without All the Anger," *Chicago Tribune*, November 28, 1999, Commentary Section, p. 19. For a report on initial reactions to Bush's executive order by some leaders in the minority community, see Sue

Schultz, "Rights Advocates Rip Florida Plan to End Set-Asides," *The Atlanta Journal-Constitution*, November 17, 1999, p. A7.

52. The statement on the agreement was found at www.flgov.com, January 2000.

53. See E. Kelly and F. Dobbin, "How Affirmative Action Became Diversity Management: Employer Response to Antidiscrimination Law, 1961–1996," in *Color Lines: Affirmative Action, Immigration, and Civil Rights Options for America*, ed. James D. Skrentny (Chicago: University of Chicago Press, 2001), pp. 87–117; L. B. Edleman, S. R. Fuller, and I. Mara-Drita, "Diversity Rhetoric and the Managerialization of Law," *American Journal of Sociology*, vol. 106, no. 6 (2001), pp. 1589–42; and F. R. Lynch, *The Diversity Machine* (New York: Free Press, 1997). Also, for a general discussion of diversity management, see T. Cox Jr., *Cultural Diversity in Organizations* (San Francisco: Berrett-Koehler, 1994).

54. The survey was conducted by the Clinton administration's National Performance Review. Data from the survey are analyzed in J. Edward Kellough and Katherine C. Naff, "Responding to a Wake-Up Call: An Examination of Federal Agency Diversity Management Programs," *Administration and Society*, vol. 36, no. 1 (March, 2004), pp. 62–90; and in Katherine C. Naff and J. Edward Kellough, "Ensuring Employment Equity," *International Journal of Public Administration*, vol. 26, no. 12 (2003), pp. 1307–36.

55. U.S. Merit Systems Protection Board, *Evolving Workforce Demographics: Federal Agency Action and Reaction* (Washington, DC: U.S. Merit Systems Protection Board, 1993).

56. Kellough and Naff, "Ensuring Employment Equity," pp. 70–71.

57. Kellough and Naff, "Ensuring Employment Equity," pp. 70–71.

58. Kellough and Naff, "Ensuring Employment Equity," pp. 71–74.

59. Trevor Wilson, *Diversity at Work: The Business Case for Equity* (Toronto: John Wiley and Sons, 1997).

60. R. Roosevelt Thomas Jr., "From Affirmative Action to Affirming Diversity," *Harvard Business Review*, vol. 68, no. 2 (1990), p. 107.

61. Thomas Jr., "From Affirmative Action to Affirming Diversity," p. 107.

62. Thomas Jr., "From Affirmative Action to Affirming Diversity," p. 112.

63. Thomas Jr., "From Affirmative Action to Affirming Diversity," p. 112.

64. Naff and Kellough, "Ensuring Employment Equity," pp. 1307–36.

65. Naff and Kellough, "Ensuring Employment Equity," pp. 1307–36.

66. In March 1996, the U.S. Fifth Circuit Court of Appeals ruled that the University of Texas School of Law could not consider race as a factor

in admitting students (see *Hopwood v. State of Texas,* 1996). The full Fifth Circuit Court of Appeals refused to rehear the case, and the Supreme Court declined to review it in June 1996. The decision was guiding law for the U.S. Fifth Circuit Court's jurisdiction, which includes Texas, Louisiana, and Mississippi. However, the Supreme Court's decision in the summer of 2003 in *Grutter v. Bollinger,* 539 U.S. 306 (2003) upholding affirmative action in higher education has superseded the *Hopwood* ruling. The *Hopwood* and the *Grutter* cases are discussed fully in chapter 6 of this volume.

67. This provision can be extended to the top quarter of the graduating class. The remaining applicants were to be selected based on criteria chosen by the individual institutions.

68. *Grutter v. Bollinger,* 539 U.S. 306 (2003).

Notes to Chapter Four

1. Richard Epstein, *Forbidden Grounds: The Case against Employment Discrimination Laws* (Cambridge, MA: Harvard University Press, 1992).

2. Cass Sunstein, *Free Markets and Social Justice* (New York: Oxford University Press, 1997), chap. 6, "Why Markets Don't Stop Discrimination," pp. 151–66.

3. For a broad defense of affirmative action based on principles of justice, see Diana Axelson, "With All Deliberate Delay: On Justifying Preferential Policies in Education and Employment," *Philosophical Forum,* vol. 9, no. 2/3 (1977–1978), pp. 264–88. See also, Gertrude Ezorsky, *Racism and Justice: The Case for Affirmative Action* (Ithaca, NY: Cornell University Press, 1991); and Michael Rosenfeld, *Affirmative Action and Justice* (New Haven: Yale University Press, 1991).

4. Howard McGary Jr., "Justice and Reparations," *Philosophical Forum,* vol. 9, no. 2/3 (1977–1978), pp. 250–63.

5. Samuel Krislov, *The Negro in Federal Employment: The Quest for Equal Opportunity* (Minneapolis: University of Minnesota Press, 1967), p. 77. Krislov attributes the metaphor to two articles that appear independently in the same journal: Richard Lichtman, "The Ethics of Compensatory Justice," *Law in Transition Quarterly,* vol. 1 (1964), pp. 76–103; and Joseph Robinson, "Giving Reality to the Promise of Job Equality," *Law in Transition Quarterly,* vol. 1 (1964), pp. 104–17.

6. *Public Papers of the Presidents: Lyndon B. Johnson,* vol. 2, 1965 (Washington, DC: Government Printing Office, 1966), p. 636. For a full discussion of

President Johnson's speech, see Hugh Davis Graham, *Civil Rights and the Presidency* (New York: Oxford University Press, 1992), pp. 98–99.

7. See, for example, Ezorsky, *Racism and Justice*; Axelson, "With All Deliberate Delay," pp. 264–88; and Amy Gutmann, "Responding to Racial Injustice," in *Color Conscious: The Political Morality of Race*, ed. Anthony Appiah and Amy Gutmann (Princeton, NJ: Princeton University Press, 1996), pp. 106–8.

8. See Sterling Harwood, "Affirmative Action Is Justified: A Reply to Newton," *Contemporary Philosophy* (March/April, 1990), pp. 14–17.

9. On the business case for diversity, see T. Wilson, *Diversity at Work: The Business Case for Equity* (Toronto: John Wiley and Sons, 1997).

10. For examples of such studies, see N.J. Adler, *International Dimensions of Organizational Behavior* (Boston: PWS-Kent, 1991); C. Nemeth, "Differential Contributions of Majority and Minority Influence," *Psychological Review*, vol. 93, no. 1 (1986), pp. 23–32; M.E. Shaw, *Group Dynamics: The Psychology of Small Group Behavior* (New York: McGraw-Hill, 1983); Warren E. Watson, Kamalesh Kumar, and Larry K. Michaelson, "Cultural Diversity's Impact on Interaction Process and Performance: Comparing Homogeneous and Diverse Task Groups," *Academy of Management Journal*, vol. 36, no. 3 (June 1993), pp. 590–602; Susan Jackson, "Team Composition in Organizations," in *Group Process and Productivity*, ed. S. Worchel and J. Simpson (London: Sage, 1992), pp. 1–12; Lisa Pelled, "Demographic Diversity, Conflict, and Work Group Outcomes: An Intervening Process Theory," *Organizational Science*, vol. 7, no. 6, pp. 615–31; and Karen A. Jehn, Gregory B. Northcraft, and Margaret A. Neale, "Why Differences Make a Difference: A Field Study of Diversity, Conflict, and Performance in Work Groups," *Administrative Science Quarterly*, vol. 44, no. 4 (December 1999), pp. 741–63.

11. Watson, Kumar, and Michaelson, "Cultural Diversity's Impact on Interaction Process and Performance," pp. 590–602.

12. Patricia Gurin, Eric L. Day, Sylvia Hurtado, and Gerald Gurin, "Diversity and Higher Education: Theory and Impact on Educational Outcomes," *Harvard Educational Review*, vol. 72, no. 3 (fall 2002), pp. 333–66. See also, Judith Butler, "An Affirmative View," in *Race and Representation: Affirmative Action*, ed. Robert Post and Michael Rogin (New York: Zone Books, 1998), pp. 155–73.

13. See "The Compelling Need for Diversity in Higher Education," Expert Testimony of Witnesses for Defendants in *Grutter v. Bollinger* and

Gratz v. Bollinger; available at www.umich.edu/~urel/admissions/legal/expert/index.html. The Supreme Court's opinions are available at *Grutter v. Bollinger,* 539 U.S. 306 (2003) and *Gratz v. Bollinger,* 539 U.S. 244 (2003).

14. Robert Post, "Introduction: After *Bakke,*" in *Race and Representation: Affirmative Action,* ed. Robert Post and Michael Rogin (New York: Zone Books, 1998), pp. 13–27.

15. Elizabeth Anderson, "Integration, Affirmative Action, and Strict Scrutiny," *NYU Law Review,* vol. 77, no. 5 (2002), pp. 1195–1271.

16. Samuel Krislov, *The Negro in Federal Employment: The Quest for Equal Opportunity* (Minneapolis: University of Minnesota Press, 1967), p. 5.

17. For a sampling of this literature, see Kenneth J. Meier, "Latinos and Representative Bureaucracy: Testing the Thompson and Henderson Hypotheses," *Journal of Public Administration Research and Theory,* vol. 3, no. 4 (1993), pp. 393–414; Kenneth J. Meier, "Representative Bureaucracy: A Theoretical and Empirical Exposition," *Research in Public Administration,* vol. 2, no. 1 (1993), pp. 1–35; Sally Coleman Selden, *The Promise of Representative Bureaucracy: Diversity and Responsiveness in a Government Agency* (Armonk, NY: M.E. Sharpe, 1997); Sally Coleman Selden, Jeffrey L. Brudney, and J. Edward Kellough, "Bureaucracy as a Representative Institution: Toward a Reconciliation of Bureaucratic Government and Democratic Theory," *American Journal of Political Science,* vol. 42, no. 3 (July 1998), pp. 719–44; Lael Keiser, Vicky M. Wilkins, Kenneth J. Meier, and Catherine A. Holland, "Lipstick and Logarithims: Gender, Institutional Context, and Representative Bureaucracy," *American Political Science Review,* vol. 96, no. 3 (2002), pp. 553–64; Samuel Krislov, *Representative Bureaucracy* (Englewood Cliffs, NJ: Prentice-Hall, 1974); Samuel Krislov and David H. Rosenbloom, *Representative Bureaucracy and the American Political System* (New York: Praeger Publishers, 1981); Grace Hall Saltzstein, "Representative Bureaucracy and Bureaucratic Responsibility," *Administration and Society,* vol. 10, no. 4 (February 1979), pp. 465–75; John J. Hindera, "Representative Bureaucracy: Imprimis Evidence of Active Representation in the EEOC District Offices," *Social Science Quarterly,* vol. 74, no. 1 (March 1993), pp. 95–108; and Julie Dolan and David H. Rosenbloom, *Representative Bureaucracy: Classic Readings and Continuing Controversies* (Armonk, NY: M.E. Sharpe, 2003).

18. The theory underlying representative bureaucracy is summarized well in Saltzstein, "Representative Bureaucracy and Bureaucratic Re-

sponsibility," pp. 465–75; and in Kenneth J. Meier, "Representative Bureaucracy," pp. 1–35.

19. For example, see Hindera, "Representative Bureaucracy," pp. 95–108; Meier, "Latinos and Representative Bureaucracy," pp. 393–414; and Selden, Brudney, and Kellough, "Bureaucracy as a Representative Institution," pp. 719–44.

20. Barbara R. Bergmann, *In Defense of Affirmative Action* (New York: Basic Books, 1996), pp. 84–85.

21. John David Skrentny, *The Ironies of Affirmative Action: Politics, Culture, and Justice in America* (Chicago: The University of Chicago Press, 1996), pp. 20–21.

22. For a presentation of this argument, see Michael Levin, "Is Racial Discrimination Special?" *Journal of Value Inquiry*, vol. 15 (1981), pp. 225–32.

23. Levin, "Is Racial Discrimination Special?", pp. 225–32.

24. D. H. M. Brooks, "Why Discrimination Is Especially Wrong," *Journal of Value Inquiry*, vol. 17, no. 4 (1983), pp. 305–12.

25. Owen Fiss, "Groups and the Equal Protection Clause," *Philosophy and Public Affairs*, vol. 5, no. 2 (1976), pp. 107–77.

26. Skrentny, *The Ironies of Affirmative Action*, p. 36.

27. See Bergmann, *In Defense of Affirmative Action*, pp. 139–41; and Skrentny, *The Ironies of Affirmative Action*, pp. 50–51.

28. Richard D. Kahlenberg, *The Remedy: Class, Race, and Affirmative Action* (New York: Basic Books, 1996), pp. 54–55; and William G. Bowen and Derek Bok, *The Shape of the River: Long Term Consequences of Considering Race in College and University Admissions* (Princeton, NJ: Princeton University Press, 1998), pp. 28–29.

29. Skrentny, *The Ironies of Affirmative Action*, chap. 3, pp. 36–63.

30. Thomas' comments were widely reported in the media at the time. For a discussion of the comments, see Kahlenberg., *The Remedy*, pp. 54–55.

31. Marc Bendick Jr., "Social Policy 2000: Affirmative Action," *International Journal of Public Administration*, vol. 22, no. 8 (1999), pp. 1213–39.

32. Bendick, "Social Polity 2000," p. 1227.

33. *Johnson v. Transportation Agency, Santa Clara County, California,* 480 U.S. 616 (1987).

34. Harry Holzer and David Neumark, "Assessing Affirmative Action," *Journal of Economic Literature*, vol. 38, no. 3 (September 2000), pp. 483–568.

35. Stanley Fish, "Reverse Racism, or How the Pot Got to Call the Kettle Black," *Atlantic Monthly*, November 1993, pp. 128–36.

36. Thomas Sowell, *Preferential Policies: An International Perspective* (New York: William Morrow, 1990).

37. These data are from U.S. Civil Service Commission, *Study of Minority Group Employment in the Federal Government* (Washington, DC: Government Printing Office, 1971).

38. Data are from the U.S. Office of Personnel Management and were accessed at www.opm.gov/ses/demograph/html, July 2005.

39. Bergman, *In Defense of Affirmative Action*, chap. 2, pp. 32–61; see also Holzer and Neumark, "Assessing Affirmative Action."

Notes to Chapter Five

1. For a discussion of this conflict of values in the context of public personnel administration, see Donald E. Klingner and John Nalbandian, *Public Personnel Management: Context and Strategies*, 4th ed. (Englewood Cliffs, NJ: Prentice-Hall); John Nalbandian, "The U.S. Supreme Court's 'Consensus' on Affirmative Action," *Public Administration Review*, vol. 49, no. 1 (January/February, 1989), pp. 38–45; and John Nalbandian and Donald E. Klingner, "Conflict and Values in Public Personnel Administration," *Public Administration Quarterly*, vol. 11, no. 1 (Spring 1987), pp. 17–33.

2. See *Firefighters Local v. Stotts,* 467 U.S. 561 (1984) and *United States v. Paradise,* 480 U.S. 149 (1987).

3. *Firefighters v. City of Cleveland,* 478 U.S. 501 (1986).

4. I would note, however, that from the perspective of a government contractor who is required to set goals for the employment of minorities and women, affirmative action is only "voluntary" in the sense that the organization voluntarily accepts the contract. From the perspective of the initiating agency, however, which at the federal level is the Office of Federal Contract Compliance Programs, the affirmative action program is entirely voluntary. In other words, the government was not compelled to impose the affirmative action program on contractors; it made that decision voluntarily.

5. Title VII originally covered only private employers with twenty-five or more employees, but it was amended to cover federal, state, and local government organizations and private employers with fifteen or more employees a few years after initial passage. Section 717, prohibiting discrimination in federal government employment was added to

the law by Section II of the Equal Employment Opportunity Act of 1972 (86 Stat. III). The 1972 Act also amended Title VII, Section 703 to bring state and local governments under the law.

6. See *Bolling v. Sharpe* 347 U.S. 497 (1954).

7. See *United Steelworkers of America v. Weber*, 443 U.S. 208 (1979).

8. *United Steelworkers of America v. Weber*, p. 205, emphasis in original.

9. *Johnson v. Transportation Agency, Santa Clara County, California*, 480 U.S. 616 (1987).

10. Because the affirmative action plan in *Johnson* was not challenged under the Fourteenth Amendment, despite the fact that a government employer was involved, the case did not address constitutional limitations on affirmative action.

11. See Lynn K. Questel, *Federal Laws Prohibiting Employment Discrimination* (Athens, GA: The Carl Vinson Institute of Government, University of Georgia, 1989), pp. 65—66.

12. J. B. Grossman and R. Wells, *Constitutional Law and Judicial Policy Making* (New York: Longman, 1988).

13. Questel, *Federal Laws Prohibiting Employment Discrimination*, pp. 68, 72.

14. Actually, the Court heard arguments in an earlier case in which the constitutionality of affirmative action was challenged. See *DeFunis v. Odegaard*, 416 U.S. 312 (1974). The Court refused to rule on the constitutional issues involved, however. Instead, a majority found that the case was moot because the petitioner, Marco DeFunis, had been admitted to law school after the litigation began. It was DeFunis' failure to be admitted earlier that had led him to file the original suit. For more on this case, see Howard Ball, *The Bakke Case* (Lawrence: University Press of Kansas, 2000), chap. 2. For text of the *Bakke* opinion, see *Regents of the University of California v. Bakke* 438 U.S. 265 (1978).

15. *Wygant v. Jackson Board of Education*, 476 U. S. 265 (1986).

16. For a more fully developed analysis of this point, see J. L. Selig, "Affirmative Action in Employment: The Legacy of a Supreme Court Majority," *Indiana Law Journal*, vol. 63 (1987), pp. 301—68.

17. *Wygant v. Jackson Board of Education*.

18. *Wygant v. Jackson Board of Education*.

19. *Wygant v. Jackson Board of Education*.

20. Justice Stevens filed a separate dissenting opinion but did not clearly articulate that the intermediate standard of review was appropriate.

21. This standard for federal government programs was later overturned

by the Court. See the discussion in chap. 6 of this work regarding the *Adarand* decision, which required the application of strict scrutiny to federal affirmative action programs.

22. See *City of Richmond v. J.A. Croson Company,* 488 U.S. 469 (1989). On the perceived impact of *Croson* shortly after the decision, see, for example, A. Kamen, "High Court Voids Minority Contract Set-Aside Program: Richmond Policy Ruled to Be Bias in Reverse," *Washington Post,* January 24, 1989, p. A1, and Mitchell F. Rice, "Government Set-Asides, Minority Business Enterprizes, and the Supreme Court," *Public Administration Review,* vol. 51, no. 2 (1991), pp. 114–22.

23. *Wards Cove Packing Company v. Atonio,* 490 U.S. 642 (1989); *Martin v. Wilks,* 490 U.S. 755 (1989). For a discussion of initial reactions to those cases, see L. Duke, "Civil Rights Activists Plan Silent Protest at Court," *Washington Post,* August 25, 1989, p. A14.

24. This point is also stressed by J. L. Selig in "Affirmative Action in Employment after *Croson* and *Martin*: The Legacy Remains Intact," *Temple Law Review,* vol. 63 (1990), pp. 1–29.

25. *City of Richmond v. J.A. Croson Company,* 488 U.S. 469 (1989), p. 752. Justice Marshall's statement is technically correct, but as noted earlier, for practical purposes, strict scrutiny was required following *Wygant.*

26. For a review of earlier cases where the courts have held that an employer's burden in a disparate impact case is proof of a business necessity, see the dissent in *Wards Cove* by Justices Stevens, Brennan, Marshall, and Blackmun, especially footnote 14 at p. 2130.

27. *Wards Cove Packing Company v. Atonio,* 490 U.S. 642 (1989), p. 2120.

28. This quote is from Justice Stevens' dissenting opinion in *Wards Cove* (p. 2136). The dissenting Justices were also troubled by the fact that employees were required by the majority to establish "practice by practice statistical proof of causation" between employment procedures and statistical disparities in the workforce (p. 2136). Justice Stevens argued that "proof of numerous questionable employment practices ought to fortify an employee's assertion that the practices caused racial disparities" (p. 2135).

29. *Martin v. Wilks,* 490 U.S. 755 (1989).

30. M.T. Larkin, "Nonparties to Employment Discrimination Consent Decrees May Attack in a Collateral Lawsuit, Decisions Made Pursuant to the Decrees," *St. Mary's Law Journal,* vol. 21, pp. 1071–73.

31. *Martin v. Wilks,* p. 2188.

32. *Martin v. Wilks,* p. 2184.

33. *Metro Broadcasting, Inc. v. The Federal Communications Commission*, 497 U.S. 376 (1990).

34. Rice, "Government Set-Asides, Minority Business Enterprizes, and the Supreme Court," pp. 120–21.

Notes to Chapter Six

1. *Adarand Constructors v. Federico Pena, Secretary of Transportation, et al.*, 515 U.S. 200 (1995).

2. *Taxman v. Board of Education of the Township of Piscataway*, 91 F. 3d 1547, 3d Cir. (1996).

3. *Hopwood v. State of Texas*, 78 F.3d 932, 5th Cir. (1996). There was a decision in the Fourth Circuit in 1994 with implications for minority scholarships at state universities. See *Podberesky v. Kirwan*, 38F 3d 147 (4th Cir. 1994). In that case, the Court invalidated a scholarship program at the University of Maryland at College Park.

4. *Hopwood v. State of Texas*, p. 394.

5. *Hopwood v. State of Texas*, cert denied, 518 U.S. 1033 (1996).

6. Sections 1981 and 1983 of the United States Code arise from Civil Rights Acts enacted by Congress after the Civil War. Section 1981 guarantees individuals equal rights under the law. Section 1983 makes state officials liable for depriving individuals of "any rights privileges, or immunities" provided by the U.S. Constitution. At issue is the constitutional guarantee of equal protection of the law found in the Fourteenth Amendment.

7. *Smith v. University of Washington Law School*, 233 F. 3d 1188, 9th Cir. (2000).

8. *Smith v. University of Washington Law School*.

9. *Johnson v. Board of Regents of the University of Georgia*, 263 F. 3d 1234, 11th Cir. (2001).

10. *Johnson v. Board of Regents of the University of Georgia*.

11. *Johnson v. Board of Regents of the University of Georgia*.

12. *Grutter v. Bollinger*, 137 F. Supp. 2d 821, E.D. Mich. (2001).

13. *Grutter v. Bollinger*.

14. *Grutter v. Bollinger*.

15. *Gratz v. Bollinger*, 135 F. Supp. 2d 790, E.D. Mich. (2001).

16. *Gratz v. Bollinger*.

17. *Grutter v. Bollinger*, 288 F 3d 732, 6th Cir. (2002).

18. *Grutter v. Bollinger*, 539 U.S. 306 (2003).

19. *Grutter v. Bollinger*, 539 U.S. 319 (2003).

20. *Grutter v. Bollinger*, 539 U.S. 318 (2003).

21. *Grutter v. Bollinger*, 539 U.S. 315 (2003).

22. *Grutter v. Bollinger*, 539 U.S. 315 (2003).

23. The majority opinion in *Grutter* provides a full examination of the *Bakke* decision [*Regents of the University of California v. Bakke*, 438 U.S. 265 (1978)]. See *Grutter v. Bollinger*, 539 U.S. 322–325 (2003).

24. See Justice Powell's opinion in *Regents of the University of California v. Bakke*, 438 U.S. 265 (1978).

25. *Grutter v. Bollinger*, 539 U.S. 329 (2003).

26. *Grutter v. Bollinger*, 539 U.S. 329 (2003) and *Regents of the University of California v. Bakke*, 438 U.S. 265 (1978), p. 312.

27. *Grutter v. Bollinger*, 539 U.S. 330 (2003).

28. *Grutter v. Bollinger*, 539 U.S. 334 (2003).

29. *Grutter v. Bollinger*, 539 U.S. 335–336 (2003).

30. *Grutter v. Bollinger*, 539 U.S. 341 (2003).

31. Chief Justice Rehnquist and Justices Scalia, Kennedy, and Thomas dissented.

32. *Grutter v. Bollinger*, 539 U.S. 343 (2003).

33. *Grutter v. Bollinger*, 539 U.S. 343 (2003).

34. See *Gratz v. Bollinger*, 539 U.S. 244 (2003). The discussion of the undergraduate admissions procedures provided here is based on the description presented in the opinion of the Court.

35. This system was modified slightly in 1996 to include only two tables, one for in-state applicants and one for out-of-state applicants. However, each cell in those tables prescribed different admissions outcomes for minority and nonminority applicants designed to advantage minorities.

36. From 1995 to 1998 the university also paced the admissions process so that a portion of seats in each entering class were held open or "protected" so that they could be filled at later dates as applications from members of specified groups came in later in the admission cycle. The groups targeted included athletes, foreign students, ROTC candidates, and underrepresented minorities. As described by the Court, "[a] committee called the Enrollment Working Group (EWG) projected how many applicants from each of these protected categories the University was likely to receive after a given date and then paced admissions decisions to permit full consideration of expected applications from these groups. If this space was not filled by qualified candidates from the designated groups toward the end of the admissions season, it was then used to admit qualified candidates remaining in the applicant

pool, including those on the waiting list." See *Gratz v. Bollinger*, 539 U.S. 256 (2003).

37. Hamacher challenged not only the system that denied him admission, but also the later policy, which he contended would prevent him from receiving equal consideration as a potential transfer student,

38. Justice Breyer also joined Part I of Ginsberg's dissenting opinion in which the Justice documents the continued problem of racial discrimination in America and stresses that the Court has not barred all consideration of race in the admissions decisions of public colleges and universities.

39. Discussions of the plan can be found in the *Los Angeles Times*, August 29, 2003; the *New York Times*, August 29, 2003; and the *Washington Post*, August 29, 2003. The University of Michigan provided a description of its new plan on a section of its website containing a substantial number of resources on *Gratz* and *Grutter*. The information was accessed at www. umich.edu/~urel/admissions/faqs/ in July 2005.

40. See www.umich.edu/~urel/admissions/faqs/ in July 2005.

41. Martin D. Carcieri makes this specific point in "The University of Michigan Affirmative Action Cases and Public Personnel Decisions," *Review of Public Personnel Administration*, vol. 24, no. 1 (March 2004), pp. 70–76.

42. Carcieri, "The University of Michigan Affirmative Action Cases and Public Personnel Decisions," pp. 70–76.

43. See, for example, Sally Coleman Selden, *The Promise of Representative Bureaucracy: Diversity and Responsiveness in a Government Agency* (Armonk, NY: M.E. Sharpe, 1997).

44. See, for example, Linda Florers and Alfred A. Slocum, "Affirmative Action: A Path towards Enlightenment," in *Affirmative Action's Testament of Hope,* ed. Mildred Garcia (Albany: State University of New York Press), 1997, p. 84. See also, Barbara R. Bergmann, in *In Defense of Affirmative Action* (New York: Basic Books, 1996), p. 10; and John David Skrentny, *The Ironies of Affirmative Action: Politics, Culture, and Justice in America* (Chicago: University of Chicago Press, 1996), pp. 87–88.

45. In addition to related works cited in chap. 4 above, see T. Wilson, *Diversity at Work: The Business Case for Equity* (Toronto: John Wiley and Sons, 1997); Jonathan S. Leonard, "Antidiscrimination or Reverse Discrimination: The Impact of Changing Demographics, Title VII, and Affirmative Action on Productivity," *The Journal of Human Resources*, vol. 19, no. 2. (spring 1984), pp. 145–75; Jonathan S. Leonard, "The Impact of

Affirmative Action Regulation and Equal Employment Law on Black Employment," *The Journal of Economic Perspectives*, vol. 4, no. 4 (fall 1990), pp. 47–63; and Robert Eugene Kasey, "Human Resource Management and the African American Worker: Research in Support of Proactive Affirmative Action Initiatives," *Journal of Black Studies*, vol. 27, no. 6 (July 1997), pp. 751–67.

46. As was noted in chap. 4, important contributions to the literature on representative bureaucracy include studies by Kenneth J. Meier, "Latinos and Representative Bureaucracy: Testing the Thompson and Henderson Hypotheses," *Journal of Public Administration Research and Theory*, vol. 3, no. 4 (1993), pp. 393–414; Kenneth J. Meier, "Representative Bureaucracy: A Theoretical and Empirical Exposition," *Research in Public Administration*, vol. 2, no. 1 (1993), pp. 1–35; Sally Coleman Selden, *The Promise of Representative Bureaucracy: Diversity and Responsiveness in a Government Agency* (Armonk, NY: M.E. Sharpe, 1997); Sally Coleman Selden, Jeffrey L. Brudney, and J. Edward Kellough, "Bureaucracy as a Representative Institution: Toward a Reconciliation of Bureaucratic Government and Democratic Theory," *American Journal of Political Science*, vol. 42, no. 3 (July 1998), pp. 719–44; Lael Keiser, Vicky M. Wilkins, Kenneth J. Meier, and Catherine A. Holland, "Lipstick and Logarithms: Gender, Institutional Context, and Representative Bureaucracy, *American Political Science Review*, vol. 96, no. 3 (2002), pp. 553–64; Samuel Krislov, *Representative Bureaucracy* (Englewood Cliffs, NJ: Prentice-Hall, 1974); Samuel Krislov and David H. Rosenbloom, *Representative Bureaucracy and the American Political System* (New York: Praeger Publishers, 1981); Grace Hall Saltzstein, "Representative Bureaucracy and Bureaucratic Responsibility," *Administration and Society*, vol. 10, no. 4 (February 1979), pp. 465–75; John J. Hindera, "Representative Bureaucracy: Imprimis Evidence of Active Representation in the EEOC District Offices," *Social Science Quarterly*, vol. 74, no. 1 (March 1993), pp. 95–108; and Julie Dolan and David H. Rosenbloom, *Representative Bureaucracy: Classic Readings and Continuing Controversies* (Armonk, NY: M.E. Sharpe, 2003).

47. *Petit v. Chicago*, 352 F. 3d IIII (7th Cir., 2003).

48. *Petit v. Chicago*, cert. denied, 124 S. Ct. 2426 (2004).

49. *New York Times*, March 27, 2004; *Detroit Free Press*, March 26, 2004.

50. For a review of the decisions by the Michigan Board of State Canvassers, see Chris Andrews, "Affirmative Action Opponents Lose Petition Bid, Plan Appeal," *Lansing State Journal*, July 20, 2005, p. 1A. For a discussion of the ruling by the Michigan Court of appeals, see Tyler Lewis,

"It's Official: Connerly's Anti-Affirmative Action Initiative on 2006 Michigan Ballot," at the website of the organization Americans for a Fair Chance at www.fairchance.civilrights.org, accessed December 29, 2005. See also "An Affirmative Action Measure Advances," *New York Times*, December 21, 2005, p. A27.

51. *United Steelworkers of America v. Weber* 443 U.S. 173 (1979); *Johnson vs. Transportation Agency, Santa Clara County, California* 480 U.S. 616 (1987).

Notes to Chapter Seven

1. There are obviously numerous books on the intricacies of social science research designs for program evaluation. Two of the more informative, in my view, are Thomas D. Cook and Donald T. Campbell, *Quasi-Experimentation: Design and Analysis Issues for Field Settings* (Boston: Houghton Mifflin, 1979); and Lawrence B. Mohr, *Impact Analysis for Program Evaluation,* 2nd ed. (Thousand Oaks, CA: Sage Publications), 1995.

2. This point is made by David H. Rosenbloom in *Federal Equal Employment Opportunity: Politics and Public Personnel Administration* (New York: Praeger Publishers 1977).

3. M. Goldstein and R. S. Smith, "The Estimated Impact of the Antidiscrimination Program Aimed at Federal Contractors," *Industrial and Labor Relations Review*, vol. 29, no. 4 (1976), pp. 523–43.

4. Goldstein and Smith, "The Estimated Impact of the Antidiscrimination Program Aimed at Federal Contractors," pp. 523–43.

5. Jonathan S. Leonard, "What Promises Are Worth: The Impact of Affirmative Action Goals," *The Journal of Human Resources*, vol. 20, no. 1 (1985), pp. 3–20.

6. Jonathan S. Leonard, "The Impact of Affirmative Action on Employment," *Journal of Labor Economics*, vol. 2, no. 4 (1984), pp. 439–63; and Jonathan S. Leonard, "Antidiscrimination or Reverse Discrimination: The Impact of Changing Demographics, Title VII, and Affirmative Action on Productivity," *The Journal of Human Resources*, vol. 19, no. 2 (1984), pp. 145–74.

7. G. E. Johnson and F. Welch, "The Labor Market Implications of an Economy-wide Affirmative Action Program," *Industrial and Labor Relations Review*, vol. 29 (1976), pp. 508–22.

8. P. Griffin, "The Impact of Affirmative Action on labor Demand: A Test of Some Implications of the Le Chatelier Principle," *Review of Economics and Statistics*, vol. 74 (1992), pp. 251–60.

9. Timothy O. Bisping and James R. Fain, "Job Queues, Discrimination, and Affirmative Action," *Economic Inquiry*, vol. 38 (2000), pp. 123–35.

10. T. Hyclak and L. W. Taylor, "Some New Historical Evidence on the Impact of Affirmative Action: Detroit, 1972," *The Review of Black Political Economy*, vol. 21, no. 2 (1992), pp. 81–98.

11. Vivian Price, "Race, Affirmative Action, and Women's Employment in U.S. Highway Construction," *Feminist Economics*, vol. 8, no. 2 (July 2002), pp. 87–113.

12. James W. Button and Barbara A. Rienzo, "The Impact of Affirmative Action: Black Employment in Six Southern Cities," *Social Science Quarterly*, vol. 84, no. 1 (March 2003), pp. 1–14.

13. L. B. Becker, E. Lauf, and W. Lowrey, "Differential Employment Rates in the Journalism and Mass Communication Labor Force Based on Gender, Race, and Ethnicity: Exploring the Impact of Affirmative Action," *Journalism and Mass Communication Quarterly*, vol. 76 (1999), pp. 631–45.

14. Kellough, J. Edward, *Federal Equal Employment Opportunity Policy and Numerical Goals and Timetables: An Impact Assessment* (New York: Praeger Publishers, 1989).

15. See Harry Holzer and David Neumark, "Are Affirmative Action Hires Less Qualified?" *Journal of Labor Economics*, vol. 17, no. 3 (1999) pp. 534–69; and Harry Holzer and David Neumark, "What Does Affirmative Action Do?" *Industrial and Labor Relations Review*, vol. 53, no. 2 (2000), pp. 240–71.

16. The quote is from Harry Holzer and David Neumark, "Assessing Affirmative Action," *Journal of Economic Literature*, vol. 38, no. 3 (September 2000), pp. 483–568; see p. 504 specifically. See also Harry Holzer and David Neumark, "Affirmative Action: What Do We Know?" Prepared for the *Journal of Policy Analysis and Management*, November 2005.

17. See Holzer and Neumark, "Are Affirmative Action Hires Less Qualified?" and Holzer and Neumark, "What Does Affirmative Action Do?"

18. The underrepresentation of women among college and university students was less of a problem. As a result, the focus has been largely on minority enrollment.

19. William G. Bowen and Derek Bok, *The Shape of the River: Long-Term Consequences of Considering Race in College and University Admissions* (Princeton, NJ: Princeton University Press), 1998.

20. This quote is obviously from the title of the work.
21. Bowen and Bok, *The Shape of the River*, p. xxiv.
22. Preferential affirmative action programs are not needed in schools that take essentially all students who apply for admission.
23. Bowen and Bok, *The Shape of the River*, pp. 9–10.
24. Bowen and Bok, *The Shape of the River*, pp. 67–68, 261.
25. Bowen and Bok, *The Shape of the River*, p. 254.
26. Bowen and Bok, *The Shape of the River*, p. 32.
27. Bowen and Bok, *The Shape of the River*, pp. 32–33.
28. Bowen and Bok, *The Shape of the River,* pp. 36–37.
29. Kane, Thomas, "Racial and Ethnic Preferences in College Admission," in *The Black-White Test Score Gap*, ed. Christopher Jencks and Meredith Phillips (Washington, DC: The Brookings Institution, 1998), cited in Bowen and Bok, *The Shape of the River*, pp. 36–37.
30. Prelim. Print. California Senate, Select Committee on College and University Admissions and Outreach, *Diversity in California Public Higher Education* (Sacramento, CA: California Senate Office of Research, May 2002), p. 7.
31. Office of the President, University of California, "2003 Freshman Admissions to the University of California, Table C, Distribution of New California Freshmen Admit Offers, Fall 1997 through 2003," *University of California News Wire*, April 16, 2003; accessed at www.ucnewswire.org.
32. www.ucnewswire.org.

Notes to Chapter Eight

1. See Michael Fix and Raymond J. Struyk, eds. *Clear and Convincing Evidence: Measurement of Discrimination in America* (Washington, DC: The Urban Institute Press, 1992). Chap. 1 of this work, "An Overview of Auditing for Discrimination," provides a good introduction to the research methods utilized and the findings.
2. In similar tests for discrimination in housing markets (both rental and sales), even more dramatic evidence of discrimination was uncovered. In these cases African Americans or Hispanics faced discrimination from 45 to 60 percent of the time. See Fix and Struyk, eds. *Clean and Convincing Evidence.*
3. For example, see Genevieve Kenney and Douglas Wissoker, "An Analysis of the Correlates of Discrimination Facing Young Hispanic Job Seekers," *American Economic Review,* vol. 83, no. 3 (1994), pp. 674–83;

and David Neumark, "Sex Discrimination in the Restaurant Industry: An Audit Study," *Quarterly Journal of Economics*, vol. III, no. 3 (1996), pp. 915–41.

4. For example, see T. D. Stanley and Stephen Jarrell, "Gender Wage Discrimination Bias?" *Journal of Human Resources*, vol. 33, no. 4 (1998), pp. 947–79; and Derek Neal and William Johnson, "The Role of Premarket Factors in Black-White Wage Differences," *Journal of Political Economy*, vol. 104, no. 5 (1998), pp. 869–95. See also related work by Harry Holzer, "Why Do Small Establishments Hire Fewer Blacks Than Larger Ones?" *Journal of Human Resources*, vol. 33, no. 4 (1998), pp. 896–914; and Harry Holzer and Keith Ihlanfeldt, "Customer Discrimination and Employment Outcomes for Minority Workers," *Quarterly Journal of Economics*, vol. II3, no. 3 (1998), pp. 835–67.

Index